Love, Jason

Doug Anderson
as told to David Williaume

Published by
Deep River Books
Sisters, Oregon
www.deepriverbooks.com

SBN - 13: 9781937756918
ISBN - 10: 1937756912
Library of Congress: 2013943347

Cover design by Joe Bailen, Contajus Designs

Now to him who is able to do immeasurably
more than all we ask or imagine, according to his power
that is at work within us, to him be glory in the church and in Christ
Jesus throughout all generations, for ever and ever! Amen.

EPHESIANS 3:20-21

Contents

Introduction

IN THE FALL OF 1974, my wife, Linda, and I enrolled in the Advanced Studies Program at Moody Bible Institute in Chicago, Illinois. One of the very first chapels featured music provided by one of the men's chorus groups, and the obvious energy and enthusiasm of one of the singers caught my notice. As the year unfolded, I saw this individual occasionally around campus but never spoke to him. At that time, I never would have guessed that one day I would be privileged to call this nameless singer my friend.

Interestingly, the student body of Moody specifically prayed for and financially contributed to the work of a Wycliffe Bible translator working in what was seemingly far-off Fort St. James, British Columbia. During that same year, God clearly directed Linda and me to key individuals, which ultimately resulted in our emigrating to take a teaching position at an isolated First Nations reserve in north-central British Columbia. Fort St. James was our nearest town and resupply point.

While in our first year of teaching, we were surprised one day by the arrival of some missionaries who had crossed the miles of lake ice to bring a Moody Science film to that reserve. Over a cup of tea, we discovered that one of the four missionaries was the Wycliffe translator we had prayed for as Moody students. We quickly formed friendships, and on our first visit to the Andersons' house in Fort St. James, we saw a photograph of the singer we had noticed a year earlier at Moody. That singer turned out to be the Andersons' son, Doug.

A few months later, the newlywed Doug and Sherrie, working through the details of responding to God's call on their lives, visited us at the isolated reserve. That initial visit led to a friendship that has spanned more than three decades.

In that time, I have watched Doug and Sherrie minister deeply to their community. When I was doing research for my PhD dissertation, I spent many hours in conversation with Wet'suwet'en people in Moricetown. The story you are about to read was mentioned by all as pivotal in the Andersons' acceptance by and ministry to the people in Moricetown. To a person, each testified that watching Doug and Sherrie walk with Christ through those difficult days powerfully impacted their lives.

It was obvious to me that this story needed to be told to a wider audience, and to that end, Doug and I have collaborated to bring you this intimate chronicle of how, as a father in deep distress, Doug learned to walk with his heavenly Father. In the writing, my faith has been challenged and enriched. I pray that in reading, yours will be also.

Dave Williaume

Prologue

MAY 4, 1980, is etched indelibly in my memory. In obedience to what we understood to be the clear call of God, Sherrie and I and seven-month-old Scott had moved from Camp Forest Springs in Wisconsin to Moricetown, British Columbia, to minister to the Wet'suwet'en First Nation peoples living there. Our mission had established a presence in the area in 1957, and we were coming to take the place of missionaries resident in Moricetown since 1966. Unfortunately, they had left before we arrived, and we found ourselves moving into a community where we did not know a single person.

It didn't take long to unload and settle our few possessions, so we spent a few days hiking in the surrounding mountains, enjoying the company of two friends and my parents, who had helped us to move. All too soon, they packed up their things and left for their homes.

We stood at the end of our driveway waving farewell and watched the dust rising from their vehicles as they headed down the dirt road toward the highway. As I walked back around the house to the pump house to see if I could get the water system running properly, all I could think was *Oh, my goodness. What have we done?*

I wanted to leave in the worst way! *I don't know anyone here! How am I going to do this?* We were supposed to go to a missionary development program, but that didn't start until September. In the meantime, we had been instructed to dive in and get to know people. Our career as missionaries was off to a shaky start.

It was there at the end of the driveway that I begin to learn to pray in earnest. I had come from a Bible church in Illinois, trained at Moody Bible Institute, and while I was big on technicalities with the Scriptures and understanding Bible stories, I wasn't big on experience in walking

with the Lord. I had no idea what I was doing, or even what I was supposed to be doing. The idea of calling out to God because I was desperate
was foreign to me, but I have come to realize that it was good for me—
very good. I had no idea how much I had to learn.

Doug Anderson

Plan to Learn More Than You Teach

DESPITE OUR UNCERTAINTY AND INEPTITUDE, we were relieved that we had made a favorable first impression in Moricetown. It had somehow become known that Sherrie's birthday came at the end of May, and a surprise birthday party was planned at the village hall. We felt truly welcomed and were enjoying ourselves and appreciative of the opportunity to meet people.

During the festivities, the elected village chief took me aside and asked me to sit down at a table with him. As we sat across from each other, he made his intentions very clear. "I don't want you to be coming here to make waves," he said, "because it won't be good if you try to separate and divide people. We don't want that around here."

I assured him that that wasn't my goal. Intuitively, I understood that the Wet'suwet'en people valued community, and his admonition was not surprising to me.

I was caught off guard by what came next. He leaned closer. "If you don't plan to learn more than you teach us . . . well, you're not going to make it around here," he warned. I mumbled a response but took his words to heart.

My opportunity to learn grew exponentially the next month when the Moricetown Volunteer Fire Department began to take shape. The Justice Institute of Canada provided intense training for the new firemen. Because the fire department was just starting, everyone involved, including the fire chief, knew very little about fire-fighting. At our practices, I was able to bond with a number of men as we learned together. This was the Lord's provision for me to begin to establish relationships with men in Moricetown.

We went to the Missionary Development Program in September and were taught that we needed to make Moricetown our home. We were advised to seek out the Christian people and live with them as the body of Christ. These should be our friends, and we should try to help each other. After we came home from MDP, we set out to do that.

My chief's words of admonition about my need to learn proved prophetic in ways I could not have imagined. Among all the things I was learning, I began to understand that God had brought me to Moricetown primarily to learn to walk with Him.

Grannie Says, "Dance"

MY MORTIFICATION WAS BUILDING by the second. Repeatedly I heard, "Doug, get up and dance!" I protested that I had never danced in my life, I couldn't dance, and that I was not going to dance. To my dismay I heard, "No, you're really supposed to. Really—because of where Sherrie is sitting. You have to get up and dance."

A girl about ten years old appeared from nowhere and dropped a blanket in my lap. She leaned over to me and whispered, "Grannie says, 'Dance!'" With that, she turned and walked away.

With burning ears, I struggled to understand what had just happened. Grannie was a well-respected elder in the community. *Uh-oh. Now I've got to dance.*

Feasts were a prominent feature of life in Moricetown, and we attended not knowing for certain whether we even should. Adding to our discomfort, the feasts were largely conducted in the Wet'suwet'en language, completely unknown to us at that time. We saw people getting up and doing things that we didn't understand. Sometimes money was collected, and sometimes groceries and other items were distributed to us. I constantly felt off balance and routinely prayed, "Lord, I really need Your help here. I'm not sure what I am doing. I'm not sure how to respond or what to say." Yet we would ask people next to us what we should do, and they would always tell us. It was a good place for us to be, because we were showing that we wanted to learn and that we wanted the people of Moricetown to teach us.

Some feasts involved dancing, while others did not. We had no idea what the pattern was or why things happened as they did. Adding to our uncertainty, in typical Wet'suwet'en expressions of humor, we were sometimes teased into doing things that resulted in laughter at our expense. Up until the blanket dropped in my lap, I would always respond the same way—"No way. I'm not going to dance."

Clutching the blanket, I nervously stood up and joined the many people from our seating section who were making their way out onto the main floor. As I followed, I asked someone what I was supposed to do. "Just wrap this blanket around you and do what we do." That first dance was truly painful. I have since danced many times, and in time it has become fun, but that first time I thought it would never end.

As we settled into life in Moricetown, I became increasingly aware that the Lord was using my experiences with a different culture to teach me things that I needed to learn. I was being forced to take the truths of God's Word that I had learned at Moody and actually live them out with these people. With the first steps of that dance, I was taking my first steps in learning to trust the Lord and to embrace new ways of doing things despite my discomfort.

What Was That About?

WHEN OUR SON SCOTT WAS THREE, Sherrie and I began to think about expanding our family. For some reason pregnancy eluded us. A battery of tests revealed that Scott's conception was surprising and that our doctor thought we weren't going to conceive again. We were disappointed, but Scott, who wanted a sibling, prayed faithfully for a baby for all of us.

Sometime later we suspected that Sherrie was pregnant, so we traveled to Hazelton, the nearest medical clinic, for confirmation. Unexpectedly, our doctor came back personally to share the test results. "I've seen two miracles since I've been working here," he said. He described one case, and then he said with awe, "This is the other miracle. From the tests that we did before, this should not be possible. You're pregnant!"

We ran from that consultation and told Scott. He was so excited that he burst out crying. At the age of five, he grasped how incredible this news was. We were all ecstatic. To add to our joy, we discovered a few months later that Sherrie was carrying twins! There was no history of twins in either of our families.

In the midst of all this, something strange occurred about which I could not make any sense. In my capacity as a missionary, I traveled extensively to visit Bible schools looking for staff for our mission's summer camp. Another mission representative and I were at a Bible school in Alberta meeting with prospective camp workers. Earlier in the trip, I had called Sherrie to see how she was doing. She said she had seen a doctor, who was considering doing an ultrasound to find out how the babies were doing. They thought they might have to send her to Vancouver, because Vancouver had better ultrasound equipment than the Smithers hospital.

That night I had a terrifying dream. I saw Sherrie lying on a table, very, very pregnant. I could see the movement of our babies beneath her skin. Suddenly, her stomach opened up and one baby leaped out to me with outstretched arms. As I picked up the baby, I saw the other baby inside of her, lifeless. I was so startled that I jumped up in bed in a panic. I realized that it was just a dream, but I remained upset. *What was that about?*

The image stuck in my mind. In my upbringing and experience, dreams were not something you normally paid much attention to. I was out of my comfort zone, intellectually and theologically, to think about that dream as something either from God or from Satan. I did not know how to deal with it, and I continued to be troubled. I prayed, "Lord, if there is some kind of curse—if there is anything in the way here—deal with it!" I also prayed, "Maybe You sent me this dream so I would pray that this wouldn't happen." I continued praying that way but didn't tell Sherrie. *It's just a dream. Maybe it's nothing. It doesn't make sense.* I kept this unsettling experience tucked away in my mind, and in the days ahead I wondered many times what it might mean.

The next morning, I got a call from Sherrie. Doctors had told her that they could not find the dividing wall between the two babies, heightening the risk of entanglement in each other's umbilical cord. In the face of this potentially serious condition, she had to go to Vancouver immediately; I had to return home as soon as possible to watch Scott. I caught a train in Edmonton and went directly back to Moricetown. The following day, Sherrie left for Vancouver, and I stayed behind with Scott. The ultrasound found the dividing wall was still intact, and the twins were fine. I was greatly relieved, though still troubled somewhat by the dream.

Michael and Jason

A SHORT TIME AFTER she had returned home, Sherrie started having back pains. I promptly drove her to the hospital in Smithers for observation. After just a few hours, the medical staff began to realize that despite Sherrie's being only seven months pregnant, she was in labor. She was admitted to the hospital to stop the labor, if possible.

With nowhere to stay in Smithers, I took Scott back home to Moricetown and put him in bed. At about three o'clock in the morning I got a phone call from the hospital asking me to come immediately. They could not stop the labor, and because the hospital in Smithers did not have the facilities to handle premature babies, they were transferring Sherrie to Vancouver. She would leave as soon as air transportation could be arranged.

Heart pounding, I left Scott with a neighbor and raced the twenty-one miles into town. When I arrived, Sherrie was being prepped for emergency surgery. "The plane won't arrive on time," medical personnel told me as I ran down the hall following Sherrie on the gurney. "The babies must come now. We're not sure if we're hearing one or two heartbeats."

With that, Sherrie and the hospital staff disappeared into the operating room. I was left in the hallway feeling abandoned. My thoughts turned to the book of Job. At the end of the book, Job had acknowledged to God, "You know what you are doing, and that is good enough for me." As I stood alone, staring through a window into the night, I prayed, "God, I want both of these babies to be all right, and I want Sherrie to be OK, and I want us to be able to just go home and everything to be fine."

As I prayed, I sensed that God was saying, "Doug, do you trust Me to do what I want to do here? Do you trust Me to do that? Can you leave that with Me? Even if it's not what you want?"

I continued, "Lord, I know I have to say—and it is the right thing for me to say—that what You want is better than what I want. I leave that with You. I put it in Your hands." Peace settled over me like a warm blanket. I said, "Lord, what I want is for Your will to be done here. Yes, that's what I want."

A few minutes later, a nurse came out and told me that I had a little baby boy. "There were two boys," she said, "but I am sorry to have to tell you that one was stillborn. We don't know why he had died, but the surviving one is fine, except for an odd little blister on his heel. We'll keep an eye on that."

Soon after this our doctor came out, put an arm around me, and asked me how I was doing. "I'm so sorry about the baby dying. I don't know what happened. Do you want to go see the baby that has died?"

I was lightheaded. I didn't know how to respond. He suggested, "Let me think this through for you. Sherrie is going to be under the effects of the anesthesia for a while. When the plane comes, both of your sons will be evacuated, and she's not going to see the baby who passed on. I think she would want to know that you have seen them both."

I agreed, and the doctor took me in to look at Michael. When I saw Michael lying there, the dream burned in my mind. He was tucked up in a fetal position, his skin a pallid blue. I was stunned—it was just like what I had seen in my dream.

I couldn't understand why God would let us have twins just to take one away. Why would He let us get all excited about having twins? Why did I have this dream? I could see no purpose in it. Because of that dream, I had prayed specifically and repeatedly for God's intervention. *And now this?*

The dream remains a mystery. Sometime later, I told Sherrie about the dream, and she is as perplexed as I.

Scott holding Jason. January 1985.

Come On Up Again!

IN THE FOLLOWING MONTHS, the loss of Michael left us with profound sadness, while at the same time we were so excited to have Jason. Because he was such a tiny guy, weighing only four and a half pounds at birth, Jason was initially sent to the hospital in Vancouver. Three or four days later, he was transferred back to the hospital at Terrace, the closest regional hospital to our home. Still recovering from the C-section, Sherrie had to stay at the hospital in Smithers through this. Shortly after Jason's arrival in Terrace, Sherrie was released, and we immediately went to Terrace to be with him.

Jason remained hospitalized in Terrace for a month. When he weighed five and a half pounds, he was released and we were able to bring him home. He had no medical problems other than being premature and starting out so small. He thrived and soon caught up in size and development. He laughed a lot, and his deep belly laughs were a delight to us all. He was a good kid—the kind who always ate his vegetables.

On Jason's first visit to my parents' house, Sherrie happened to notice a crumpled note lying on the floor beside a wastebasket. Wondering what it was, she opened it and read, "Are you willing to trust God for whatever comes into your life, even if you never understand why?" She tossed it into the wastebasket, even more perplexed by the strange dream.

We hadn't expected ever to have more children, yet we had twins and lost one. Because of this, I told Sherrie that I wouldn't be surprised if God gave us another child. God did exactly that. To our delight, seventeen months later, another son, Matthew, was born. Matthew was a daring, adventurous boy who did everything with reckless abandon.

Jason holding Matt. Summer 1986.

Being so close in age, Jason and Matthew developed a special relationship. Occasionally, they would manage to get into trouble together.

Jason and Matthew had been afforded the privilege of sleeping in
bunk beds, which I had built for them. Jason was on the top bunk, Matthew on the bottom. One night just after we put them to bed, I heard
Jason call down the hallway, "Dad, Matthew is in my bed." Because he
was younger, Matthew wasn't supposed to be in the top bunk bed.

I went into their bedroom and, sure enough, Matthew was in the
top bed. I said, "Matthew, you're going to fall off of there. I do not want
you up in that bed."

Matthew agreed, and I put him down in his bed. A few minutes later
I heard Jason call out, "Dad, Matthew is back in my bed again."

I went down there yet again and I said, "Matthew, if I come down
here again because you disobeyed me, there will be a spanking!"

I had scarcely left the room when again I heard Jason call, "Dad, Matthew is in my bed again." I was genuinely puzzled as to why Matthew was
so blatantly disobedient. I returned and gave him a mild reprimand and

put him back in his bed, but this time I only pretended to leave. Instead, I stood just around the corner and listened. I heard Jason say, "OK, Matt, come on up again!"

At this, I stepped around the corner and told Jason, "This is the rule, right here. Every time Matthew is in your bed, you both get spanked." That ended the reports of Matthew in Jason's bed.

Jason wasn't perfect, but he was a lot of fun to be around. He enjoyed being outdoors, and particularly hunting and fishing. We had the opportunity to fish in northern Ontario when Jason was three years old. He would go out in the boat with us and take his turn reeling in fish that I or another adult had hooked. Although he thought that was fun, he wanted so much to catch a northern pike. Because he was so young, he couldn't cast more than a few feet from the boat. Despite this, he kept casting all three days. Finally, at the end of our stay, he caught a northern pike right beside the boat, all by himself. Jason was persistent.

When Jason was five years old, we vacationed on Haida Gwaii as a family. Each morning and evening, I would take either Scott or Jason deer hunting with me, and during the day, we would relax and play together as a family. Early one morning, as we were quietly moving through a clear-cut, Jason whispered behind me, "Dad!"

I turned around. Jason was staring at something. Standing above him on a gravel cut bank was a little button buck. I whispered, "Stand still." Jason froze, clutching his BB gun. The little buck came out onto the road, and as it started walking toward him, Jason slipped his gun to ready, one leg back of the other. The little buck came right up to him and stuck out his nose to sniff at him. I will never forget the picture of Jason and this deer—two little bucks standing face-to-face, unsure what to do or think.

What Do You Want?

IN APRIL OF HIS EIGHTH YEAR, Jason started complaining that his right arm hurt him near his shoulder. It especially hurt when he threw a ball at school. When the pain continued, we took him to the doctor. The initial medical opinion was that it was a strain and that, given a little time, it would heal.

However, time did not bring any relief. Sometimes I noticed him working his hand a little bit, and I could see that his shoulder hurt. While never excessive, the pain was always there.

Things continued this way for a couple of months, but we were not overly concerned. The pain in his arm did not seem a great hindrance, and in every other way Jason seemed healthy. We concluded that it was something that would just take some time to get better.

Near the end of June, Jason went with his class to the pool at Smithers. While he was swimming, his arm suddenly hurt him a great deal—so much that he had to stop what he was doing. We immediately took him to the doctor's office to get his arm checked out.

The way the X-ray technician studied the film bothered me. In my experience, X-ray technicians verified that the image was of good quality, but I sensed that there was something more.

We were told that some irregularities were present, and that the film would be sent to Prince George for reading by a radiologist. We gave our consent, and Jason's arm was put in a sling. With no idea of the seriousness of the situation, we went home to prepare for family camp at Rock Nest Ranch.

At family camp, Jason's arm continued to give him great discomfort, and he had trouble sleeping at night. Because of his constant pain, instead of attending the camp meetings, he and I went for walks to take his mind off his arm.

That Sunday morning during the service, I again took Jason to a quiet place where we could be alone. As we waited in one of the staff houses, we found a Bible storybook. I sat down with him, and looking out the window over the camp property, read him the story of Jesus sleeping in the boat. When a fierce storm blew up, the disciples thought they were going to die. In a panic, they woke Jesus up. Jesus spoke to the storm, and all became quiet.

I talked with Jason about how Jesus is always with us, just like then. I stressed that Jesus is always in the boat with us, no matter what. Eventually we could see that the camp meeting had ended, so we went down and joined everyone for lunch. Following lunch, we had a baptismal service for Daren, a relatively new believer.

A certain woman was upset about Daren's getting baptized. There were a few things she thought weren't right in his life, and because of these things, she strenuously opposed his baptism. We talked to her about her concerns, but she remained adamant.

Despite her objections, that afternoon we baptized Daren on the basis of his confession of faith. Afterward, we packed our things and returned home to Moricetown. The next day, Monday morning, we had scheduled a follow-up appointment for the results of the X-ray reading in Prince George.

Jason's arm gave him much pain that night, and all we had to give him for pain was aspirin. He slept out on the floor in the living room, and Sherrie and I lay beside him, trying to comfort him in any way we could. About the time he finally fell asleep, the phone rang. It was the woman who had objected to our baptizing Daren. She was at a bar and had been drinking. She told me that she had gotten upset at us because we had baptized Daren, and because of that, she went out drinking. She said that her drinking was our fault. Then she said, "I wasn't going to tell you this, but I'm going to. I have this gift, and I know when bad stuff is going to happen to people."

She told me of several incidents around Moricetown, including the death of a young baby. She said, "I knew that was going to happen. I don't know how, but I just knew that was going to happen." Then she said, "I'm just calling you now to tell you, for whatever it's worth, I've got a real black feeling about your son Jason. Something bad is going to happen to him."

This upset me, especially because we were still waiting for the specialist's report. I retorted, "I don't think that is a gift from God. For one thing, you're telling me this from a bar. You're drinking. I don't think that is a gift from God."

She said, "Well, whatever. That's just what I think is going to happen."

Even though I didn't think that this was a message from God, I was in turmoil. I did not tell Sherrie immediately what the call was about. Instead, I hung up the phone and went into my office. I stood there, terrified, in the dark. I leaned on the windowsill and stared into the backyard, wrestling with my emotions and with God. I prayed, "Lord, what is going on? Why did she call me? Why did she say that? I'm scared. I don't know what is going on!"

As I was speaking to the Lord, John 15:7 came to mind. "If you remain in me and my words remain in you, ask whatever you wish, and it will be done for you". At that moment, I felt like the Lord was saying to me, "What do you want, Doug?"

I said, "Well, Lord, I know that I don't abide in You perfectly—by far, I don't. But I believe You abide in me."

I sensed that the Lord continued to say to me, "Well, what do you want?"

I responded, "Well, right off the top of my head, what I want is for Jason to be OK."

But then I began thinking of Solomon and how he answered the Lord when confronted with a similar question. Solomon answered with wisdom. *OK, what I really want, what I really want, deeply, is that Jason wouldn't just be OK. More than anything, I want that Jason and our entire family would know that You, God, are everything that You said You are. I want that we would know and see that You are good, powerful, and faithful—and that the people around Moricetown would see it. That's what I want.*

That has to be better than just asking for Jason to be OK. It can't be wrong to ask that. I asked God to do this because I thought that was the best thing that I could ask for.

That was a very special, deep time—I will never forget the experience, the verse, or any of it. After that time in my study with the Lord, I felt like I should go right in and tell Sherrie what had just happened. I walked out into the living room and did exactly that.

Jason was lying asleep on the floor by the couch; Sherrie and I sat on the floor near the woodstove. After I told her everything, we got on our knees right there by the woodstove and prayed, "Lord, we commit this whole thing to You. We don't know what is happening, but we commit it to You." With that, we went to sleep ourselves.

What's the Matter, Dad?

THE NEXT DAY, I took Jason into Smithers to find out what the doctors in Prince George had discovered. "I'm sorry," the receptionist said. "The doctor can't see you right away. You can probably see him in an hour or so. You might as well pick up Jason's codeine prescription while you wait."

Codeine? That really set me back. Codeine is a powerful painkiller. Why would she say that? Pick up codeine? We haven't even seen the doctor yet. I was so upset that when I met people I knew on the way to the pharmacy, I couldn't hear what they were saying. I began to realize something was wrong. *This isn't right!* Shock was setting in.

When we returned to see the doctor, Jason was asked to stay in the waiting room while I was invited to the examining room. I felt like I was sliding into a nightmare. Terror gripped me as I sat down and waited for the doctor to speak.

"Look, there is no easy way to say this, so I'm just going to say it," the doctor began. "Jason has cancer. We don't know what kind, but it's serious. It's in his arm. The reason his arm hurts is because it broke in the swimming pool. You have to get him down to Vancouver as soon as possible. I don't recommend that you drive because you're not going to be in any shape to drive that far. I know this is hard to hear. You can just sit in this room for as long as you need to. I'll go and give you some time alone."

I probably looked like I needed some time alone. I felt like someone had just kicked the wind out of me. I could not fathom what I had heard.

The doctor walked out of the room, and I sat there, stunned. I don't remember praying. I don't remember anything.

After a while I, took a deep breath. *I've got to go home. I've got to get Jason and go home.* I stumbled out of the examining room and down the hallway to the waiting room. Jason was sitting there in his chair, kicking his feet, not touching the floor. He was only eight years old.

I was overwhelmed. I wanted to fall apart, but I couldn't let myself. Barely holding it together, all I could think was that I had to get home— I had to get Jason home. When I reached the waiting room, I felt like everyone was looking at me. I grabbed Jason by the hand. "Come on, Jason. We've got to go."

I led him a few feet down the sidewalk, turned left, and started to walk down an alley the opposite direction from where our car was parked. Jason tugged at my hand. "What's the matter, Dad?"

"Nothing's wrong. I'm just acting silly, that's all." I knew that wasn't a very good answer, but that's all I could think of, and it seemed to satisfy him for the moment. We eventually found our car and drove toward home. On the way, we passed a cliff where just a couple of weeks before I had taken Jason on an overnight campout. I looked up at that rock outcropping. *Oh, man. I'm just going to explode.*

Somehow I made it home without falling apart in front of Jason. Once inside our house, I left him in the living room watching TV. I grabbed Sherrie, and we hurried back into my small office. She sat down in the only chair and waited for me to speak. I totally came apart, and she pulled me onto her lap and held me like a baby. I couldn't speak, so she began to ask me yes-or-no questions so that I could at least nod my head.

Eventually I started to get things a little under control. "Jason has cancer."

"Is he going to die?"

"No, they didn't say that, but because they don't know what kind of cancer it is, we have to go to Vancouver right away."

Sherrie just held me. "It's going to be OK," she said. "It's going to be OK."

That was the beginning of a long journey that would take us to a place we could never have imagined. In the days ahead we were to discover that sometimes Sherrie would fall apart like that, and I would hold her and tell her that it would be OK. Then, as on this day, there were times she would do the same with me. Very seldom did we both fall apart at the same time.

Now We're Going to Learn to Swing From the Rope

SHERRIE IMMEDIATELY CALLED our neighbor and good friend Chris and told her we had to go to Vancouver. "Don't tell everyone about this right now," Sherrie said, "but Jason has cancer. We have to go to Vancouver right away. We have to line up a flight. We don't know if we're going to drive or what. I don't know if we have money to fly down."

True to her Wet'suwet'en culture, Chris knew this was not a burden to be carried alone and had no intention of keeping it quiet. Within an hour, our house was filled with people from Moricetown. Our driveway was jammed with vehicles, and the overflow spilled out up and down the road. People brought food for the streams of friends who arrived. Some served coffee and snacks, some sat with us, and everyone left money on the kitchen table—just piling bills up in a heap.

A few weeks previously, I had been moved by God to challenge our church to trust God completely. I had used rappelling as an example. When you rappel, you really sense that your whole life is hanging on the rope. I had said that trusting God is like when you go off a cliff—you have to put your entire weight on the rope. Daren, the one I had baptized a few days earlier, had heard my challenge that day and made immediate connection to our circumstances.

I was in the driveway when I met him. Daren grabbed my hand and pressed money into my palm. Then he hugged me. As he embraced me, he said, "Doug, now we're going to learn how to swing. Now we're going to learn how to swing from that rope."

Daren's words proved to be prophetic. As a new Christian, Daren was about to become the leader of Kyah Fellowship, because I would be gone from Moricetown. From that point on, I was going to be hanging on to the rope by the skin of my teeth—the rope of the things that I believed, or said I believed, about God and eternity.

There Will Be Four

THAT NIGHT WE DECIDED to fly, because the money that was given to us more than covered the cost of tickets to Vancouver. Amid the confusion, we did two additional things that night. Jason had brought two little pine trees home from school, and I had not yet taken the time to plant them. When I saw them sitting, roots wrapped, on the kitchen counter, I thought we should plant them before we left.

As a family, we slipped out into the backyard. As we planted those seedlings, I prayed that the trees would grow to be tall and strong, and that Jason would too—that God would do both of those things.

After we planted the two seedlings, we went into the house. Sherrie and I realized that we had not yet told Jason what was happening. We took him into our bedroom, away from the crowd, and dealt with this second important thing. We said, "Jason, this is what is going on. The doctors think you have a disease, cancer, and it's pretty serious. We need to go down to Vancouver, right away. We're going to go on the plane tomorrow." I went on, "You don't need to worry, because it's going to be just the three of us. All three of us are going down. It will be the three of us in the plane."

Jason smiled up at me. "No Dad. Remember the story you told me yesterday? There will be four of us."

Sherrie and Jason on the first flight to Vancouver. June 29, 1993.

Easter Seals House

THAT NIGHT WHEN MOST PEOPLE had left, we had a special time of prayer with my mom and dad. We all held hands, prayed about the testing that was coming up, and committed it all to the Lord. Sherrie, Jason, and I were on the first plane out of Smithers to Vancouver the following day.

On the plane ride down, I don't know whether Jason was scared or could sense that we were. Personally, I had no idea what we were walking into, and I was terrified.

In Vancouver we took a taxi to Children's Hospital. We didn't know where the oncology department was, and when we walked into the lobby everyone was running around, and we had no idea what we were doing or how we should go about doing it. Eventually we found out where we needed to go. We filled out preliminary paperwork and then were sent to the chemo outpatient area. We walked into a room filled with kids—some with no hair, others missing limbs. Most were getting chemotherapy and looked very, very thin and sickly. It was crowded, busy, and overwhelming. We were directed to a waiting room to await our turn for some preliminary testing.

One of the first tests was a CT scan. Jason was laid on a table; I was not allowed to stay with him. I went into another room where the technician worked and watched over his shoulder. I didn't know what I was looking at, but I was scared to death of what I might see. I saw an ominous shadow between his lungs. "Is that a tumor?" I asked the CT technician.

"No, that's his heart," the technician replied. I decided to wait outside.

For at least the first three days, I forced myself to eat but had absolutely no hunger. I was so upset and scared about where we were and what was happening. The hospital had directed us to the Easter Seals

34

house, and every day we walked the short distance from there to the hospital with Jason.

One day shortly after our arrival, we were waiting to see a doctor to get further test results. As we sat in the hallway, we overheard a doctor talking heatedly on the telephone. Among the bits and pieces of the conversation, he said, "I can't go out there and tell them that....Just because you saw a couple of little spots...I can't be giving them news like that!... That sounds so hopeless when we're not sure....I'm not going to do that."

With a sort of pity, I wondered who that guy speaking on the phone was, and whom he was talking about.

The doctor came out and saw us sitting there. He must have realized that we had overheard his telephone conversation. The uncomfortable expression on his face confirmed he was Jason's doctor and had been talking about us.

Spots.

Hopeless.

He tried to make it sound like things were looking good but that we needed to do a biopsy to see what kind of cancer Jason had so the best treatment could be applied. Finally, he told us that they had found spots on Jason's lungs, indicating that the cancer might have spread there as well. They weren't 100 percent sure, but they thought it had. In the days ahead, I came to think of that particular doctor as an executioner. I hated to see him because I feared what he was going to tell us next.

The next several days continually brought bad news. It took a few weeks to find out what kind of cancer it was. That wait was extremely hard. It was so difficult to know that Jason had cancer, and yet we couldn't begin doing anything about it because we first had to find out what kind of cancer it was.

One night, Jason was having particular trouble sleeping because of the pain from his still-broken arm. We gave him a painkiller. Because he couldn't sleep lying down, we propped him upright in a corner with pillows. We were surprised that he actually fell asleep that way. That night when sleep finally came, Sherrie and I got on our knees beside the bed where Jason was propped up, and we started to pray.

Until that moment, I had never prayed with Sherrie like that. We prayed for Jason, and we prayed for Scott and Matthew, who were back in Smithers with my mom and dad. As we brought all these things before the Lord, we were literally at the throne of God. Time disappeared. We didn't want to stop, because we both sensed that everything was really OK.

The Pay Phone

BEFORE WE FOUND OUT Jason had cancer, I had been going out to Fort Babine regularly hold Bible studies and see an elderly friend, George. Our visits often led to long discussions, with a usual theme being George's objections to Christianity. His favorite topic was the problem of evil—if God is a God of love, why does He let little kids suffer? George contended, "God can't be a God of love with all the suffering I see happening in the world—kids suffering like they do." None of our explanations or counterarguments could dissuade him.

With our sudden turn of events, Sherrie and I found ourselves stranded indefinitely in Vancouver, guests at the Easter Seals House. Our only means of communication with people was through the pay phone down in the basement. About two weeks after we arrived at Easter Seals House, I was speaking with a friend from home on that pay phone. He said, "I went up to visit George, and I told him about Jason. Doug, he accepted the Lord."

I was dumbfounded. *George accepted the Lord?* I would have expected George to say, "See, I told you." The Lord worked in his heart and somehow softened him, and instead of lashing out, his response was that he wanted to follow Christ. *Lord, You work in strange ways. You work in really strange ways.* The very thing that would be good ammunition for George to fire back at me was what the Lord used to save him. I don't understand George's logic, but the Lord knows.

Curiously, that pay phone became special to me. I used it to speak to an old friend, Pastor Krenz, whose wife had died of cancer. In that conversation he said, "You may not like what I am about to say, but I think that what will help you is to start thinking about a thousand years from now. It will help you to put into perspective what you are going through right now. What will it be like a thousand years from now? How will you look back on this time a thousand years from now?" He went on, "I believe the Bible teaches that we will be thanking God for what He has put in our lives right now."

That stuck in my mind. I realized that I was fixed on the immediate—my world had fallen apart and I couldn't see past today. This pastor friend affirmed that what had sustained him through the things he had endured with his wife was realizing that a thousand years from now, he would look at all of this and say, "Praise God for what You did in my life. Praise You for how You blessed me with every single thing You did." That was a special call on a special pay phone.

Terror or Trust?

IN THOSE FIRST WEEKS, life was more stressful than anything we had ever experienced. We went to the hospital every day for testing and soon discovered that the tests to determine the type of cancer Jason had were terribly painful. Jason's pain was unrelenting, and it became an ongoing struggle to get him quieted down and relatively comfortable so he could sleep. After Jason drifted off, Sherrie and I would get down on our knees and pray as we had never prayed before. We prayed conversationally, and night after night poured our hearts out to the Lord. We sensed that the Lord was present and real. In these times of prayer, a resolve grew that no matter the outcome, we wanted to stay in this deep experience of God. We wanted to learn to walk with God like this when things were back to normal.

We had experienced some tough times as a family. As we looked back to some of these hard times, we developed new perspectives. We began to express to each other how we would love to go back to some of those hard times now. In the moment, things had seemed so horrible, but we now recognized that those times were nothing compared to our current circumstances. We began to regret that we had not been more thankful in those earlier times. As we reflected, the realization grew that God wanted us to be thankful right now. We kept thinking about Pastor Krenz's admonition to keep focused on the end of the story, and how, when we see the whole picture, we will be thankful for what God has done. We resolved to be thankful right now in our present circumstances.

We had to remind ourselves of this resolution continually. As time went on, we would fall back into the pattern of thinking that was focused on the present horrible circumstances. We would have to bring ourselves up short and admit to ourselves and to God that we were doing it again and needed to be thankful for our present circumstances. As we did this repeatedly, our perspective changed. We began to realize that God's grace really is sufficient to cover any situation. We began to realize that, from our perspective, difficult times are pretty much all equally difficult at the time they are experienced. It is hard to compare them and say that one is more difficult than another.

God's promise to Paul that His grace was sufficient means that whatever circumstance you are in, God's grace is equal to that circumstance. We began to realize that God's grace makes all circumstances doable because God goes through the experience with us. Even though I might feel I am at the lowest depth, God's grace brings me way back up to the top again. The further down I am, the more recognizable it is that it is God who has lifted me up and given me strength. It is always God's strength—but that fact is more obvious when I am way down than it is in better times. I believe that is why God has us go through those very, very difficult times.

During this time the Lord began to teach me about trust. I have found that it is easy during good times to say that you trust Christ with your family, but when everything is pulled out from under your feet, things feel quite different. When we dedicated Jason and our other sons as babies, we thought we were giving our children to the Lord. At the time, we were being as honest as we could. Through the act of dedicating each of our sons to God, we were saying, "He's in your hands, Lord." However, as we battled Jason's cancer, I came to realize that I was really saying, "Yes, he's in the Lord's hands, but really, we are watching over him. We are protecting him." I came to realize that God took Jason out of our hands and allowed him to have a disease that I couldn't fix. The outcome was entirely in God's hands. When that happened, my response was terror. Feeling helpless in the hands of God, my first response was terror, not trust.

When you're in the shallow end of a swimming pool, it is easy to say that you aren't afraid of deep water. If you're wearing a life jacket, you may quite readily say that you know this life jacket will hold you up, even in the deep end. But when you find yourself thrown out into the deep end, only then do you find out how much you actually believe. In my terror, a shocking realization confronted me: "Lord, I don't trust You as much as I thought I did."

Through Jason's cancer, I began to understand that the Lord was saying to me, "You can trust Me. I want you to understand what that means—I don't want you just saying words." Before Jason's cancer, I was not lying when I said that I trusted the Lord. In saying that, I now realize that I was unaware of how little I actually did trust the Lord. Through this difficult time, God was saying to me, "You can trust Me with everything. You can trust Me totally."

Ewing's Sarcoma

IT TOOK SEVERAL WEEKS before we got the report back from the initial biopsy. It is an understatement to say that the wait was nerve-racking. As we approached the end of our wait, Jason was admitted to the hospital and given a place in a four-bed ward.

When I was eight years old, my teacher shared with the class about visiting a leukemia ward. She described how sick the children were and how skinny they looked. This triggered a phobia in me that lasted well into my junior high years. I feared death, and I feared disease—especially leukemia. My fear was debilitating. Some days I was so afraid of that kind of death that I could not eat. My stomach was racked with pain, and I wondered if that pain was itself a symptom of the disease I feared.

As I entered high school, I began to seriously read the Bible for myself. I became challenged to God's truth through my youth group at church. For the first time, I began to grasp the significance of Proverbs 3:5–6:

> Trust in the LORD with all your heart
> and lean not on your own understanding
> in all your ways submit to him,
> and he will make your paths straight.

I responded as best as I could by consciously putting my trust in God and walking with Him. Now, years later, I found myself sitting beside Jason in a room with four beds—three of the children had leukemia, and my eight-year-old son had an as yet unidentified form of cancer.

Finally, the report came in. We were ushered into a conference room and sat down. Across the table was a grim-faced team. We were told that Jason had Ewing's sarcoma, a rare form of round-cell cancer often associated with bone, and that he had about a fifty-fifty chance of survival. The road ahead of us would be very, very difficult.

The doctor recommended that our family relocate to Vancouver immediately and told us that we could not expect to return home often. "This will be a very difficult time for your family," he said. "What is ahead of you often breaks up families. It will take great effort for your marriage to survive. You will have to work hard to keep your family together, and it's vital that you try to live as normally as possible."

I reeled with shock. Voices sounded distant and unreal. After the doctor left, a Christian nurse stayed behind and prayed with us. We really appreciated that. When she finished, we walked out into the hallway, intending to head back to Jason, who was waiting in his room.

The week before we found out that Jason had cancer, a very good friend of mine, John, had moved to Vancouver. We had been so sad to see John and his wife, Marge, go and had no idea then that we were going to be following them such a short time later. We would soon discover that their presence and a gift John had given to us would prove to be God's special provision.

Just before we reached Jason's room, there in the hallway was John. He could tell by looking at us that the news was bad. Still in shock, I told him a little bit of what we had just been told. Immediately he responded, "Well, we should pray!"

I agreed, and we slipped into an empty chapel just outside the 3B cancer ward. Sherrie, John, and I sat down. "Well, we should pray," John said again.

"John, you know what?" I replied. "I don't think I can. Could you pray?"

John said he would. But his silence stretched out longer and longer. *Uh-oh. I shouldn't have asked John to pray. That is a big load—he's a new Christian. I shouldn't have done that.*

I was wrong. John wasn't afraid; rather, true to his culture, he was sitting in silence as he composed his thoughts. Only when he knew precisely what he wanted to say to God did he begin to pray aloud. I couldn't tell you the exact words that he prayed, but I remember it was so good. John prayed not only exactly what I needed to hear, but exactly what I wanted to say to God even though I could not find the words. It was an amazing experience to listen as John prayed my heart to God.

A Thousand Shall Fall at Your Side

BESIDES JOHN'S PRESENCE, another thing that helped me in those first weeks was a musical album that he had given me. In the months before John had moved to Vancouver, he had attended a Steve Bell concert in Smithers. There he had purchased a cassette tape for himself and one for me. He had given me the cassette with the condition that I had to listen with the volume turned up. I think he wanted to be sure I paid attention to the lyrics.

I did really listen to the lyrics Steve sang. In fact, for that first month in Vancouver, the Lord used the songs on that album to sustain me. The songs based on Psalm 90 and Psalm 91 became particularly precious to me. I grabbed on to the lyrics based on Psalm 90:

> Satisfy us in the morning with your unfailing love,
> that we may sing for joy and be glad all our days.
> Make us glad for as many days as you have afflicted us,
> for as many years as we have seen trouble.

Steve's rendition of the Lord's Prayer spoke powerfully to me. Years later he returned to do a concert in Smithers. In the intervening years, we had not listened to that recording because there was such emotion tied to it. I simply couldn't play it—it was too much for me to hear it. At this concert, Steve again sang Psalm 90. A flood of emotions overwhelmed both Sherrie and me. After the performance, I made my way up to talk to Steve. I told him, "Steve, you are never going to know how powerfully God used you in my life. At a time when I was so low, God used your music to touch me so deeply."

Casually, Steve replied, "Oh, I'm glad to hear that."

I thought perhaps I hadn't expressed myself well enough. I wanted to grab him and shout, "No! You don't get it! It's more than that."

During the weeks following Jason's diagnosis, Sherrie and I were driven to read and reread Psalm 91. This psalm affirms that a thousand will fall at your side, ten thousand at your right hand, and circumstances won't touch you. Pestilence, deadly arrows—they won't touch you, so, you don't need to worry. On one particular day, this was of such encouragement to me that I began to tell Sherrie about it. She replied, "Yeah, but it sure looks like it has touched our tent." I had to admit—it did look that way.

As I continued to reflect, I struggled to understand the promise. It seemed like deadly pestilence had touched our tent and that a thousand were falling at our side literally. We saw sick kids dying at the hospital, and our son faced the same prospect. This dissonance marked the beginning of my deeper understanding of this Psalm. I began to see the connection between Psalm 91 and something that Jesus said to His followers in Luke 21:12–18. In verses 12–17, Jesus warned his followers that some of them were going to face persecution and trouble and even die. With this as the context, in verse 18 Jesus made a shocking promise: not even one hair on their heads would be lost.

As I thought about these two passages, I began to see that Psalm 91 and Luke 21:18 were talking about the same thing. It won't touch your tent. Not a hair of your head will perish. You are safe. I began to connect these passages with what Pastor Krenz said about a thousand years. I began to realize that in a thousand years we would look back and be able to say, "It never touched our tent. Our son was OK the whole time. Thousands perished around us, but look! We are all safe. The Lord brought us through it—all of us!"

I believe that we do ourselves a great disservice in speaking of a physical sense as somehow separate and opposed to a spiritual sense. I have come to understand that both come together and join in one reality. There is only a real sense. In a real sense, in reality, it does not touch your tent.

The Lord was promising to see us through this difficult thing, and He did. He truly did. He saw Jason through it, and He saw us through it, and He still is. Psalm 91 is not a promise that if you become a Christian, you won't have to worry about diseases or even attacks of the enemy. It means that you don't have to worry about it, not that you won't see it. It promises that when you see it, you can have this absolute confidence that God is with you, and He is going to bring you through it. You can rest right in the middle of the storm.

We began to connect this to Psalm 84, which talks about how the saints of God turned the desert places into a spring, with pools of water. All this happened because they came to recognize how God had taken care of them in the midst of things that seemed to be horrible. In reality, God was taking care of them. We were learning to rest in the reality that God was taking care of us.

I Don't Want to Live Anymore

WE STAYED THREE WEEKS at Easter Seals House. As it became more apparent that we would need to live in Vancouver for some time, we were advised that Ronald McDonald House was better structured to meet our situation. We visited Ronald McDonald House and were impressed with the leadership and the staff.

Despite our needing a place to stay, at that point I wasn't interested in moving to Ronald McDonald House. I didn't want to face other people—I just wanted to be alone. What I didn't realize at that time is that these people were going through what we were going through, and because of that, we would deeply bond.

Shortly after we moved into Ronald McDonald House, a little boy who had previously lived there came back. It seemed to me like everybody was going out of his or her way for this child. I wasn't opposed to that, but he seemed relatively healthy. One day, a big limousine came and picked him up. *What's the deal? What's with this guy? There are so many kids here who are sick, and he's getting all this special treatment.*

This sick young boy knew many of the kids there, and we were newcomers. With all his special treatment, I resented him. As far as I could see, he didn't seem to be all that sick. After he left in the limousine with his folks, I asked the manager, "Who is that kid?" The manager told me his name and continued, "They are sending him home to die."

That hit me. Instantly I felt awful for how I had been thinking about him. It was the worst thing that I could think of—they were sending him home to die! I did see him again about six months later, and he was almost unrecognizable. Shortly after that he did die.

This incident was one more step in my realization of the difficult things that other people were facing. Everyone tried to put the best foot forward, so to speak, but still it was difficult. We found this to be true of ourselves as well. When we started our treatments with Jason, we were told that it was going to be rough. Jason was going to have a three-day round of chemotherapy, three weeks off, and a second five-day round of chemotherapy, followed by another three weeks off.

This doesn't sound bad at all.

That was my ignorance speaking.

We soon came to realize that the treatments would make Jason so sick that in his times between treatments he would rarely get to go home. It would take him three weeks to recover from the effects of the few days of chemotherapy. As we went through those first three weeks, we watched Jason throw up continually and lose all of his hair. It is impossible to describe how traumatic that was. Because Jason couldn't eat anything, he started losing weight rapidly. If we could get him to eat a cracker for the day, we were doing well. Jason became weaker by the day. Walking became difficult and climbing stairs impossible.

We made it through the first cycle of chemotherapy, and at the end of the three weeks off, just as he started feeling a little bit better, he went into five days of chemotherapy. This led to another three weeks of sickness, with Jason never feeling well enough to have left the hospital. Those first six weeks were unspeakably difficult. The doctors told us it might get better as Jason's body got accustomed to the poison of the chemotherapy, but that never happened. Jason sank into a deep depression. It seemed like he was giving up. Even though he didn't say it, you could read it in his eyes—I don't want to live anymore.

The Picnic Bench

AFTER THE INITIAL SIX WEEKS of chemotherapy, we went to the doctors and told them that we had to get Jason out of the hospital for a break. The doctors consented and gave us a three-hour pass. With great expectations, Sherrie and I took Jason down from his hospital room and put him in the car. He always liked to go to Stanley Park, mainly because it was the most natural outdoor environment he knew in Vancouver. We drove out to Stanley Park with him perched uncomfortably on a cushion between our bucket seats.

As we turned into Stanley Park, Jason started to complain of a pain in his back. His discomfort increased, and he started to cry. As Jason screamed in pain, all we could think was that the cancer had spread to his back. In a matter of moments, Sherrie and I became upset with each other, even yelling at each other, while Jason cried nonstop. Our greatly anticipated oasis time became a descent into an abyss.

I turned the car around and drove directly back to the hospital. Since Jason was unable to walk, I carried him to his room. We told the hospital staff what had happened, and arrangements were made to investigate the source of his pain. By then I was so upset that I left Jason on the bed and headed toward the door. Sherrie asked, "Where are you going?"

I said, "I don't know. I'm just leaving." I did not handle things well at all. Sherrie was mad at me, and I was mad at her. I did not understand at the time, but our anger with each other was simply our response to the stress of the situation.

I went downstairs and out through the front door of the hospital. It was about five or six in the evening, and the sun was setting. I noticed a picnic table off to one side, so I went over to it and sat down. I was boiling with anger at God, and I began to rail at Him and vent my frustration with Him. I recounted to the Lord what we had experienced so far. "Jason had a pain in his arm, and we prayed that it wouldn't be anything serious. It was *cancer*. Then we prayed that it wouldn't be a bad kind of cancer. We found out that it was a very bad kind of cancer, *Ewing's sarcoma*. We prayed that it wouldn't spread, and we found out it *had spread*. So then we prayed that he would be able to handle the chemotherapy treatments. The doctors said he almost had an allergic reaction to it—*worse than most kids*. You want me to pray about stuff, but everything I prayed about has gotten worse than expected. Now, do You want me to pray that Jason's back won't be anything serious? I don't know if I want to do that anymore, because it doesn't matter what I pray—You just do what You want to anyway."

I didn't hear an audible voice, but at that moment, I felt like the Lord said, "You're finally getting it. You're starting to really get it. That is true—I do whatever I am going to do." The passage that Sherrie and I had chosen as our life verses when we were in high school came to mind. They were the verses that had become precious to me in high school and had set me free from my debilitating fear of leukemia—Proverbs 3:5–6. As I thought about it, I realized that these verses were saying almost the same thing. I began to understand that in these verses God was saying to me, "I do whatever I am going to do. That is why you need to trust in Me with all your heart, and not lean on your understanding. In all your ways acknowledge Me, Doug, and I will set your paths straight. I will guide you through this. But you have to trust Me."

In that sacred moment, I understood those verses as I never had before. Before this encounter with God, I had understood these verses in a superficial way. I am not sure what I thought trusting the Lord with all my heart even meant. Now I understood that these verses are saying that *when life doesn't make sense, and you don't know what God is doing, trust Him*. Even when you can't figure it out, He knows what He is doing. Rest in that, and if you do, He will direct your steps. This proved to be a very important lesson and sustained me in my dire situation.

I felt like the Lord met me there on that picnic bench in a real, deep way. I didn't feel light, or happy, or that everything was good. I was still bowed under a load of overwhelming grief, but I had calmness in my spirit that I didn't have before I sat down at that picnic table. I was able to walk back into the hospital and up to the ward to see Sherrie and Jason.

Not long afterward, we found out that the pain had been caused by a muscle spasm in his back, triggered from lying in bed so long. The pain in Jason's back wasn't anything serious. My unvoiced plea had been answered—God met me and was teaching me to trust Him even when I didn't know what He was doing.

Of Daughters
and Boats

RONALD MCDONALD HOUSE in Vancouver is a modified old mansion. People living there occupy the bedrooms and share bathrooms. Because sick children live there, everyone must be incredibly clean and careful. For example, after you take a shower, you must wipe the walls down and sterilize every surface. Consequently, Ronald McDonald place is immaculate.

After we had been at Ronald McDonald House for a while, a couple moved in with their little girl. She was seven or eight years old and had just been diagnosed with leukemia. The dad wore a blank look on his face. I recognized that look all too well. It was like he was not even there—people would talk to him, and he looked past them. I knew just what he felt like. He was in shock—he couldn't believe that his daughter could possibly have a disease like that.

Later that evening, I went into the TV room downstairs and saw this man sitting alone in the corner of the room. The TV was on, so I sat on another couch to see what was playing. I looked over at him; he was staring over the top of the television set without seeing the screen.

"How are you doing?" I asked him.

"Not very well."

I asked him a few questions about his daughter, and then he began to talk like he was voicing his innermost thoughts. "I am from Vancouver Island. I'm a used car salesman. I don't have a lot of money, but one of my passions is an old sailboat. With my spare time and spare money, I've been fixing up that sailboat. I go down there every chance I get, and I build this, clean that, add here, and do whatever. That sailboat was my pride and joy." His voice began to break. "I see my little girl here. I would give everything I have for her to be OK. It's all coming into perspective for me. That sailboat is just a pile of garbage. I spent way too much time on it. I can't believe I was so stupid."

"I understand what you're saying," I replied. "When I brought my boys to Vancouver, after I found out about Jason, we bought things like roller blades and took time to do things as a family in a way we never did before. My oldest boy, Scott, even commented to Sherrie, 'What's got into Dad anyway? He never used to spend money like that.'"

I had an urgent desire to spend time with my kids. I wanted to do things with them. I realized that I might not have them as long as I'd thought. That's what this dad was coming to understand.

We had a heart-to-heart talk. I even shared about my hope and trust in the Lord, and he was open to hearing it. I can't say that he became a Christian, but we did have a good discussion.

Later, his daughter did die.

Such was the level of relationship we developed with people at Ronald McDonald House. On many occasions, Sherrie and I engaged in conversations about real, deep things with people—right away. In this case, I was with this man for fifteen minutes, and he was sharing the depths of his heart with me. Our shared circumstances quickly drove us from the superficial to what really mattered.

A Pig in the Ward

ONE OF THE STRANGE THINGS that first struck us about living at Ronald McDonald House was how freely parents talked about the morbid details of what their kids went through—sometimes with laughter. After being there for a little while and going through some of the same things they went through, we began to understand why they were doing that. They needed somebody to talk to who would understand. They understood each other, because their kids were going through same things. Almost always there was some parent there whose kid was just hanging on, barely alive, and they didn't know if their child were going to make it. As time went on, it seemed that we took turns being in that position. Chemotherapy would adversely affect the children's immune systems, leading to potentially fatal infections. At Ronald McDonald House, you were always surrounded by people who understood, and it was therapeutic to talk about it.

We met a number of memorable kids at Ronald McDonald House and grew close to them as we got to know them and their parents. Particularly memorable was a boy named Andrew. Andrew didn't have cancer, but he had another terminal disease. On Halloween, he came downstairs dressed up as a Power Ranger. I played along.

"Whoa! It's Billy the Power Ranger."

Andrew was nodding his head like he was saying, "Yeah, that's me all right."

"Is there any chance, Billy, any chance at all, that I can get your autograph?" I handed him a piece of paper

He put an A on the paper for Andrew. He finished the A and said, "Oops." He crossed off the A, grabbed my shirt, and pulled me down so we were face-to-face. "How do you spell Billy?"

The attachments we formed with these kids at Ronald McDonald House were life shaping. A year after meeting Andrew, I attended his funeral, still surrounded by other sick kids, hoping against hope that all of them, including Jason, would make it. The effect is profound not only on the sick children and their families, but also on the hospital workers who serve these children. One incident powerfully illustrates this.

One evening as I was watching television with Jason in his hospital room, I heard a blood-curdling squeal come from a nearby room that sounded much like a pig in distress. I went out in the hall, but I couldn't see anything. Assuming the staff must have taken care of any problem, I returned to watching television with Jason. About an hour later, the floor nurse came in. We had a great relationship with this particular nurse, so I said, "I've got to ask you a question. I heard this squealing sound. What were you guys doing? It sounded like a pig."

She got a sheepish look on her face. "Don't tell anybody, but it was a pig." She explained that there was a little boy in the next room who would probably be dead in the next couple of days. She had been talking to him and had asked him if there was anything he wanted to do. He had replied that he always wanted to pet a pig and never had a chance to do so. Although it was against all the hospital rules, this nurse had some-how located a piglet. The blood-curdling squeal we heard was the piglet's protest at finding itself in a hospital room, being petted by a sick child.

Am I OK?

ONE OF THE THINGS that concerned me was that Matthew might ask me if Jason was going to die. That eventuality bothered me a great deal, because I didn't know what I would tell him. Matthew was seven years old, and I vainly hoped he wouldn't ask me. As I wrestled with this in my mind, I knew that I did not want to say, "No, he's not going to die," and I did not want to say, "He might." I had absolutely no idea what to say.

One day, without warning, Matthew posed the dreaded question. Even as he asked, I still had no idea what I was going to say. I was walking with him and Scott back to where our car was parked. Jason was really sick at that time, and as we walked, Matthew came right out and flatly asked, "Dad, is Jason going to die?"

In that moment, God gave me the answer. I turned to Matthew, I reached out my hand, and I said, "Matthew, look at this. What if this were God's hand? In God's hand are Mom, you, Scott, me, and Jason. All five of us are in God's hand. Of our family, who is safer in God's hand?"

Matthew replied, "We're all safe."

"Yes!" I said. "So Jason is just as safe as you are, and as safe as I am, because we are all in God's hand."

Matthew replied, "Oh, OK." And that was it—he was satisfied with that answer. We continued to walk. *Wow. That is it! That is true.* I hadn't thought of that analogy before Matthew asked me, but when he asked me, it was there. God gave me that answer, but not even a minute ahead of time.

Really resting in this truth has not been easy for me. God has used a variety of means to help me learn to rest. When Jason was in for treatments, Sherrie and I alternated staying overnight in the hospital with him, and we both spent many nights on that roll-out bed. Sometimes I felt OK, but often those were times when, going to bed, I would feel overwhelmed with everything. One particular night as I lay on the roll-out bed beside Jason's bed, I was overcome with anxiety.

Someone had given us a Ricky Skaggs album as a gift. As I lay down, I put on the headset and began listening to this new tape. The last song on the album was "Somebody's Praying."

That night, God ministered deeply to me through that song. As I listened, I could sense the reality of what the lyrics described. The song went on to talk about angels watching over me, and then it affirmed that I could go on because of the prayers of God's people. As the song concluded in an expression of thanksgiving, I realized this song spoke of my real condition—there really were countless people praying for us. It was overwhelming for me. God used that song to encourage me that night, and it remains a special song for me.

On another night, I was in a similar state of mind. This time Jason had a private room, which we had come to realize was not something you wanted. Although the privacy was nice, you got a private room only when things were bad—and things that night were really bad. After everyone else had left, I lay crying on the roll-away bed. *Maybe Jason's not going to make it, even now. Maybe he's not going to make it.* I poured out my heart to the Lord. I told Him, "Even here, You could just say a word, and Jason would be better. He could just walk out of here. All You would have to do is to say, 'Be better!' I don't understand why You don't."

That night I felt God was saying to me, "Doug, it is enough just to know that I could do that. I could do that, but I am not. But you go to sleep, because I could do that, right now." That thought hit me in a way that it had never hit me before. I stopped asking, "Lord, why aren't You?" I understood that the Lord was saying to me, "Isn't it enough to know that I could? I could, and I am right here. I am right beside you, and I am right with Jason. And you guys are OK. Now, go to sleep."

I began to understand that my kids were looking to me for assurance. Many times, Jason would look to me and say, "Dad, am I OK?" I learned that in turn, I had to look to God and say, "Dad, am I OK?" That night it was as if God were saying, "Doug, I could fix it all, right now. Yes, you're right. I could. That's enough for you to know. I am right here, all the time." That night I did experience incredible peace. I just went to sleep and slept well.

In the days ahead, I discovered that when I conveyed this message to my kids, they felt at peace. They looked to me as Dad and asked, "Am I all right?" I would have to look to God and ask Him the same thing. I would hear Him say, "Yes, you are all right," and I could then honestly answer my kids. It was such a simple, yet profound, thing that I needed to learn.

The Illusionist

A NUMBER OF PEOPLE were touched by Jason's situation. Among them was one of Jason's favorite teachers from his Christian school back home. This teacher loved illusion, and he came down Vancouver to attend an illusionists' international conference. This teacher knew that Jason also loved illusion, so, to our surprise, he hired a well-known illusionist who was attending this conference to come to Jason's room and give him a special magic show.

I have been impressed by illusionists from time to time, but never so much as by this man. Despite his wearing a short-sleeved shirt and working with his back to me as he faced Jason, he made objects show up and disappear at will. He also brought a box of tricks, which he gave to Jason. As he worked his way through the box, he first showed Jason how the trick would look when you did it correctly. Then he would break the trick down into steps as he showed Jason how to perform it. He spent more than a half hour with us. When it was time to go, I noticed that he left the hospital without stopping to visit any other room. I wondered what this was all about.

I was still wondering when I got a call from Jason's teacher. He said, "I've got to tell you something, Doug. I hired this illusionist to come to Jason's room. I purchased the gifts, the trick box, and I hired him to come to the hospital and put on a show for Jason and teach him how to do the tricks. I wasn't going to say anything to you, except now I have to. The illusionist just called me and told me that he didn't want any money for what he just did. He said it blessed him to do that for Jason."

The Letter

IN THE FIRST MONTHS in Vancouver, our world had turned upside down. Literally overnight, we were uprooted from our rural home and moved to cosmopolitan Vancouver with Jason. Sherrie and I didn't return home to Moricetown for months; for Jason it was to be sixteen months. We knew almost immediately that we were going to need to live in Vancouver for some time—our problem was that we had no way even to guess for how long. As it turned out, the initial twelve months of chemo took sixteen months because the treatments were so devastating to Jason's body.

After we had been at Ronald McDonald House for a month or two, the director met with us. He told us that we were welcome to stay as long as we wanted, but they had found that it was better for families to rent a house rather than staying with them long term. We immediately started looking for a house to rent and were able to find a place in Surrey not far from Children's Hospital. Because we couldn't get immediate occupancy, we continued to stay at Ronald McDonald House.

A new school year was starting, so we enrolled Scott and Matthew in local schools they would attend after we moved. Because of the distance involved, this meant that for several weeks Sherrie or I had to take the boys to and from school every day. The commute could be very time-consuming, so often I stayed out in Surrey all day and waited while they were in school.

Sometimes I would go to a park to pray and be alone. On one particular day, I brought along an unopened letter from Pastor Krenz, my retired pastor friend who lived in Wisconsin. With his letter and my Bible in hand, I found a bench in a remote place where I could look down over a small valley. I opened my friend's letter and began to read.

He wrote, "I was out jogging this morning, and I saw a dead robin lying on the road. I thought of you. The reason I thought of you is because of what Jesus said—not a sparrow falls to the ground apart from His will. God knew that robin. He knew when it was going to die and that it would die on that road. That's how intimate God is to His creation. Now either Jesus was exaggerating or He knows you, where you are, and what you are going through. Not a single thing will happen to you apart from His will. You need to choose to believe that today."

My friend, so far away, had no way to know that this was the very thing I was struggling with. I greatly respected this man and knew that he had lost his beloved wife to cancer. I had to consider his words carefully. As I sat there looking at his letter, I dropped my hands and glanced up. In a bush directly in front of me, not more than three feet away, I saw a sparrow sitting on a branch. As I looked at that sparrow, I prayed, "God, you placed that bird right there." It was as if the Lord was telling me, "There it is, Doug. Look! I put this sparrow right there for you. It won't fall to the ground apart from me. I love you even more than I love that sparrow, right now, even in all of this."

In response I said to God, "Yes, I believe You. I believe You." It was a small incident, but one of the many times I sensed God saying over and over to me, "I am with you, and I know where you are. I know what is going on in your life, and I am in control. So you can rest."

Where's Matthew?

THE TRANSITION TO A NEW SCHOOL proved more difficult for Matthew than for Scott. Considering everything, Scott did well. Matthew, however, being only seventeen months younger than Jason, was deeply troubled and affected by the things Jason was going through. Matthew worried about his brother, and when he saw Jason crying, he became unnerved.

Because the cancer was in the bone in Jason's shoulder, the doctors felt that the best course of treatment was to surgically remove the affected tissue. The plan was to administer three rounds of chemo to knock the cancer back, remove the bone, and follow with more chemo. We could either remove the arm entirely or try to remove the affected joint and fuse the bones back together. This would leave Jason without a movable shoulder joint, but with an otherwise usable hand and arm. We chose the second option. The discovery of spots on Jason's lungs led to the decision to increase the second cycle to twelve months' duration. We were told the surgery was major and would likely take fifteen hours.

The day came when Jason was to go back to the hospital for the surgery. When we told Jason it was time to go, he screamed at the top of his lungs for at least five minutes. I held Jason on my lap as he shouted over and over, "No! I'm not going to do it!"

Eventually he calmed, and I told him, "Jason, I would cut my own arm off, gladly, for you to not have to do this. But that won't help you. You just have to trust the Lord for this. If there was anything else we could do, I would do it. But this is what the doctors feel is the best thing to do." To this, eight-year-old Jason acquiesced, "OK."

We took Jason down to put him in the car, but when we called his brothers, Matthew was nowhere to be found. We searched everywhere.

Eventually we found Matthew curled up in a ball under his bed with his hands clenched over his head. Little Matthew could not handle what was happening to his brother. Before Jason had gotten sick, Matthew was utterly fearless; in fact, he often scared me with the things that he would do. From the time he was a toddler, he would routinely climb up on high furniture and leap off, expecting me to catch him. Matthew abruptly changed in Vancouver. He became very cautious; the world for him had suddenly become very dangerous.

We Are Earnestly
Praying for You

WE HAD BEEN PRAYING INTENSELY that Jason wouldn't need this surgery. If it were successful, it would cripple him; he would lose the shoulder joint in his right arm. In the worst case, Jason knew that he might not be able to use his hand at all after the surgery. Over and over, we asked God to heal him miraculously so this surgery wouldn't have to be done. But God did not choose to heal him, and we resigned ourselves to the necessary surgery.

Upon our arrival at the hospital, we were given a private room in the surgical wing rather than the cancer ward. The surgery was scheduled for the next morning. As we were settling down for the night, Jason asked me if I would read him a Bible story.

Earlier, I had started reading to Jason directly from the Bible rather than just telling him the Bible stories. Even though he was eight years old, I found that if I chose good narrative passages, he would follow along and enjoy it. That night we were understandably nervous. When Jason asked me to read from the Bible, I tried to think of a good passage that I had not already read. As I thumbed through my Bible, the Lord brought me to Acts 12, the story of Peter's release from prison.

At this point in the Acts narrative, James, John's brother, had already been killed. When they had seized Peter and put him in prison, they turned him over to four squads of soldiers to guard him. As Peter was kept in prison, the church was praying earnestly for him. I stopped right at that phrase and said, "Jason, the church is praying for you right now. Many churches are. They are praying earnestly for you right now, that God will set you free from this cancer, and that God will help us."

Unexpectedly, the phone rang. I gave the Bible to Sherrie and asked her to finish the story. I answered the phone and began to talk to an individual I had never met who attended a Bible college in Surrey that I had never visited. This perfect stranger began, "My name is José. I am at a prayer meeting right now, and we heard about your son being in the hospital. As we were having our prayer meeting, the Lord laid it on my heart that I had to call you and tell you that we are earnestly praying for you right now. I don't usually do things like that, but I sensed so strongly that God wanted me to call you that I felt like I would be sinning if I didn't call you right now. So, for whatever it is worth, we are earnestly praying for you right now. I wanted to call you and tell you that."

I was astonished. I hung up and told Jason about what José had said. Jason casually replied, "Oh. That is good!"

I am convinced the call was for Sherrie and me. In a stranger's voice, we heard God encouraging us once again, "I am with you. I know what is going on." Through that call, God gave us peace.

Hand in Hand

THE NEXT DAY, JASON was in surgery for fifteen and a half hours. We appreciated that some people came and sat with us during that day, and the call from José continued to give us real peace. We were able to leave Jason in God's hands.

This day reminded me again of an image I remembered from the day Jason had his initial biopsy. As on that day, we could accompany Jason only partway before we were met by staff. We reached the point where we handed Jason over to the doctor. Standing there, we watched our little boy put his hand into the doctor's hand and watched the two of them turn and walk down that hall together. In that moment, I realized again that I had to trust that doctor totally. Jason's life literally was in his hands. As I watched them going down the hallway, the Lord was showing me a picture of how I also was putting my son into His hands. Through Jason's cancer, I was learning to say to God, "I can send him with You, because I know he is safe with You." I was coming to understand that God was saying to me, "You *can* do this. Put your son in My hands. I will take him, and he will be OK." That day I trusted Jason into the doctor's hands, and, just as certainly, I entrusted him to God's hands.

That image came back into my mind many times over the next months and years. I would picture Jason with his hand in God's hand and see them walking down the hall together. *It is OK. God is going to take care of him. He is OK.* I would often feel like I had to be there for Jason, that I was the one whose responsibility it was to protect him. I came to understand that God was saying, "No, you can't do that at this point."

After the fifteen and a half hours of surgery, Jason recovered in intensive care. We were allowed to go in one at a time and see him as he woke up. Jason looked like the Michelin man, all wound in bandages. He was huge around his chest with just his hand sticking out of the bandages and some pins sticking out of his shoulder. He could only whisper because of the anesthetic.

When it was my turn to go in and see him, the first thing he said to me was, "Dad, look at my hand." I looked and saw that he was wiggling his fingers. We both understood—God had answered that prayer with a "Yes!"

The following weeks were difficult for our family. Once the bandages were removed, the pins had to be cleaned several times each day, which was excruciating for Jason. At last, the day came when the pins could be removed. We were all so excited about that. The doctors were very pleased with how the surgery went and how he was healing. When they removed the pins, they told Jason and us that it was very important that he did not break that fusion. The chemotherapy reduced his ability to heal, and if he broke his arm, it likely would never heal again.

We were very careful. Bone used for the graft had been harvested from his leg, so Jason was stiff and in constant pain. As a result of bone harvesting, Jason's toes curled up tight. This led to yet another surgery to release the tendons in his toes so he could extend them again. Jason had to learn to walk again. Initially, he used a cane to support himself.

One day, despite Jason's being so careful, we noticed that his shoulderless arm didn't seem right. It had too much movement and was swollen. But he wasn't in pain, so with everything else that was going on, we were not overly concerned and gave it no further thought.

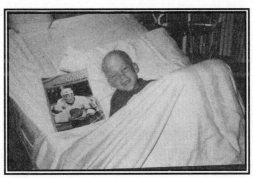

Jason in Children's Hospital in Vancouver. The presence of the trays indicates that he was undergoing chemo at the time. Spring 1994.

Broken Again

THE FOLLOWING WEEK, Jason was going back to the hospital for another round of chemotherapy, so we waited until then to take action regarding his arm. We mentioned the situation to our doctor, who immediately examined Jason and ordered X-rays. We then settled into our room so Jason could rest as much as possible.

A short time later, my good friend John came to visit. John and I went for coffee in the cafeteria at the hospital, and we talked about the relationship between David and Jonathan. We compared our relationship to theirs. As we talked, Jason's orthopedic surgeon walked in to the cafeteria and came over to me. This was not normal, and as soon as I saw him, terror broke over me. I knew something was wrong.

He said, "Doug, could you come over here a minute so I can talk to you?" *This is bad.*

The doctor said, "We got the X-rays back. Jason's arm is broken. I have no idea what we are going to do about it. It likely will not heal again, and it might swing like that the rest of his life, with no stability. If that happens, I don't know that the arm would ever get strong. It needs to be stressed to be strong, and if it remains swinging free, it would atrophy." He continued to explain that he didn't expect that the bones could ever grow back together. "I don't think we should tell Jason, because he doesn't need any more stress in his life right now. It's not hurting him because that bone is grafted into the harvested leg bone, and there are no nerves attached to it." We'd already discussed other options such as another painful, dangerous surgery. "I advise you to just leave it that way, but I will do whatever you want. You are the parent."

The doctor left, and I told John what he had just told me. John and I had a significant, deep time of praying together, just the two of us.

After we prayed, I called Sherrie. As we talked about it on the phone, we decided that Jason had to trust us and to know that we wouldn't hold out on him, but that we would tell him whatever we knew. Even though he was only nine years old, we would tell him.

I started to go upstairs to tell Jason. John said that he would pray for me but that he had to leave. John and I prayed again, and as we were parting, he said he would continue praying for me as I talked with Jason. As I headed upstairs, I didn't have a clue what I was going to say to Jason, other than "The doctor told me your arm is broken."

When I got to Jason's room, the curtain was closed, and it was dark. I got on my knees beside his bed so I could be eye to eye with him. "Jason," I said, "your doctor just talked to me and told me that your arm broke."

As soon as I told him that, Jason started to cry. He knew what it meant. "I tried to be careful," he sobbed.

"Jason, the doctor said that he knows that you have tried to be careful and that you have not fallen. He said that the bone is smaller than a pencil. Just leaning on it with a cane was probably enough to snap it."

As I listened to Jason cry, God reminded me of the story of Job. "Do you want me to tell you a story from the Bible?" I asked. Jason said he did. I began to tell the story of Job in an abbreviated way and read selected parts of the narrative aloud from my Bible. At the end of the story, I said to Jason, "When God appeared to Job in the whirlwind, what do you think God was trying to tell him?"

Jason thought a minute. "I think he was trying to tell Job, 'I know more than you do.'"

I asked Jason, "What was Job's response?"

Jason replied, "Well, Job realized that God knew more than he did, and everything was OK."

"That is exactly right, Jason. That is what God is telling you and me right now." It was one of those incredible times with my son, because in sharing the story of Job, I was sharing with him where I was too. Both he and I were there. "That is what God is telling us right now. He knows what He is doing. To us this sounds like bad news, but I think God wants us to thank Him for what He is doing and just to trust Him. Maybe we should do just that right now."

Jason said, "OK."

We both prayed right there. We thanked God for the broken arm and that He was in control and that He knew what He was doing and that everything was going to be OK. As soon as we finished with that prayer, Jason said, "Hey, Dad, do you want to watch *Rescue 911* with me?" As far as Jason was concerned, the matter was done and settled. With everything settled, why not watch TV? It was such an incredible thing to see.

We did not know that God was about to do something that would amaze both our doctors and us. Without treatment or a cast or a splint, the bone spontaneously rejoined, and in time, became strong. Jason's shoulderless arm became anchored, and it did not atrophy. There was no medical explanation. God chose to do it.

Routine

WE SETTLED INTO A ROUTINE. Jason was confined to the hospital for chemo treatments for weeks at a time and then returned home for a few days to recover for the next round. Either Sherrie or I would be at our rented house in Surrey when Scott and Matthew were not in school, and the other would be at the hospital with Jason. Most days, Scott and Matthew came to visit Jason. Sherrie and I alternated, with one of us spending the night in the hospital, sleeping beside Jason on a little roll-away bed, while the other slept at our house in Surrey with Scott and Matthew.

I had to learn to do another thing that was difficult for me. Jason's medication had to be administered by injection every day, and in order for him to be able to come home those few days for rest, I had to learn to give him the injections. I hated doing it, because the thick fluid caused him extreme pain.

Jason became very ill from the chemotherapy. Often for a week or two at a time, he would vomit nearly once an hour. The numerous monitor leads and intravenous attachments, combined with the damage done to his leg in harvesting bone for the shoulder graft, made doing anything a challenge, and getting to the toilet even more so. These were miserable days for all of us.

During the rounds of chemotherapy, Jason would literally go a couple of weeks at a time without eating. He was getting nutrition and hydration from the IV, but despite eating little or nothing, he continued to vomit nearly continuously. A feeding tube was installed through his nose, but it had to be removed because his vomiting kept dislodging it. Eventually, yet another surgery was performed, and a feeding tube was installed directly into his stomach. That was an improvement, although infection set in, which caused further pain.

Jason had continuous battles with infection. Despite all preventative efforts, his chemo injection port sometimes became infected; occasionally it collapsed and needed to be replaced. It took time for the replacement port to heal, and because it was vital that the chemotherapy treatments not be interrupted, temporary ports would be installed in his groin. In the process, a wire was inserted into a vein, and to verify that the correct vein was entered, run up to Jason's heart. Once it was confirmed that it was in the right place, the doctors would install an injection tube that would go up into the large vein. This procedure was done under conscious sedation.

One particular time, Jason asked me to stay with him through the procedure. That was a hard thing for me to do. It was no comfort to remind myself that he would not remember what happened. Before giving his consent to my presence, the doctor had warned me that the procedure was a difficult thing to see. Before he began the procedure, the doctor told me to kneel or be seated. He didn't want me to stand up because he said he didn't want me passing out and falling down. Despite this warning, I still was not prepared for what I saw. Although sedated, Jason seemed to be far more conscious of what was going on than I thought he would be. He clung to me, and as I watched the doctors searching for the correct artery, I was so glad that I had been told to kneel.

Throughout the procedure, I just kept praying, "Lord, help me not to faint, not to pass out here." They finally finished, and after it was over Jason was taken back to his room to recover. Although Jason had no memory of the ordeal, I was exhausted.

NHL All-Star Game 1994

THIS PARTICULAR TEMPORARY PORT PROCEDURE was performed just a few days before the 1994 NHL All-Star Game, which was being hosted by Vancouver. We could usually get tickets given to us for events, so before this unanticipated procedure, we had obtained three tickets and had planned for Jason, Scott, and me to attend. After this procedure, we were told that we could go, but we had to make absolutely certain that Jason remained in a certain exact position in the wheelchair. The temporary port could easily rupture the vein it was placed in, and if that happened, Jason would bleed to death in minutes. Despite that dire warning, they said he should be all right and they thought he could do it.

Needless to say, I didn't feel good about the situation. I went to the doctor and said, "Jason and Scott really want to go to that game. I do too, but I only have three tickets. Would you be willing to use my ticket and take Jason and Scott to the game? I would feel so much better knowing that a doctor is right there with them in case something went wrong." The doctor thought about it a second, and said, "Yeah, I think I could do that."

About ten minutes later, a nurse who had overheard my request to the doctor came into our room. "That doctor just bugs the heck out of me," she said.

"What do you mean?" I asked.

She said, "Oh, he sat in this room with you, pretending to think for a minute before he said, 'I guess I could do it.' You don't know it, but he walked into the staff room after you did that, jumped up on top of the table, and was dancing, saying, 'I'm going to the All-Star game! I'm going to the All-Star game!' Don't think for a minute that he is doing you a favor!"

The nurse was mistaken—he really was doing us a favor. He was great with the boys and somehow got them in to see Don Cherry, which made Scott's day. During the All-Star game broadcast, while providing his usual color commentary, Don made a remark about rooting for a little guy in Vancouver who was going through some hard times. Without a doubt, Jason was on Don's heart and mind.

John and Marge

JOHN AND MARGE BECAME very special people to us. Somehow, they seemed to "just happen" to visit us at critical times. John was with us when we were first told that Jason had a fifty-fifty chance of living through cancer. That was the first time I realized how serious this was. I walked out of that meeting, and there was John—standing in the hall. Another time was when we got the news that Jason's arm had broken. In yet a third critical time—there was John, again.

Jason did not respond well to chemotherapy. He seemed overly sensitive to many drugs, and because of that, he was normally administered a half dose of one particular medication. On this occasion, Jason had a different attending physician than he normally had. Somehow, this doctor was not aware of Jason's sensitivity to this drug, and consequently, he administered a full dose. Almost immediately, Jason became immobilized. Worse yet, he started to vomit without being able to move. In minutes, he became paralyzed from the neck down.

Sherrie found a nurse and reported this situation but was told this is a normal response. Sherrie knew it was not normal, so she persisted. "I want you to come into this room, and I want you to sit beside this bed for half an hour. Just sit there."

The nurse came and saw that Jason was looking straight ahead, not responding. Then he threw up without moving a muscle and started to cry. The nurse realized that something was very wrong, so she ran down the hall and found a doctor, who immediately responded.

Just as this incident started to unfold, Marge and John happened to stop by to drop off a gift. It was around 3:00 p.m., and although they had not planned to do so, they stayed until about 1:00 a.m. They sat with us to see us through, and it was so precious to have them there. The doctors took Jason off all medication, and he eventually came out of his reaction. It was a terrifying experience for us, and more so for Jason, who was paralyzed and unable to breathe properly. Once again, the Lord had John and Marge come just when we needed them.

All of us, including John, noticed this. He said, "It's uncanny. It's not like we are here all of the time."

I began to sense that God was making a disciple out of John and was using me in this process. I hadn't realized it before because I was too buried in what was happening. I was just trying to survive as a Christian, and John was trying to help me. Together we both learned to walk with the Lord. This situation with Jason was an effective classroom where John and I learned about trusting God.

To this day, I have a heart connection with John. When we get together, we have an instant bond and can talk about deep things right away. I think that is what God meant when He told us to make disciples. Without a doubt, Bible study and knowledge of God's Word is important in discipleship. We did those things, but everything came together experientially in these desperate situations we kept finding ourselves in. In that process, we were being discipled together. Together, we were learning to trust God.

Lana

TIM AND LANA WERE an energetic young couple serving with a sister ministry to ours. Lana took on serving Jason and our family as part of her personal ministry. She would come regularly to sit with Jason and, in so doing, allow us much-needed time to run errands or simply decompress. As she sat with Jason, she got to know him well. Jason loved to have Lana come.

That last statement is significant, because Jason was selective as to whom he allowed to get close to him. He welcomed his grandpa and grandma and his great-grandpa, but very few other people were allowed close to him. Lana was one of the privileged few—she found favor in Jason's eyes.

Lana referred to Jason as her boyfriend, and he loved it. The incongruity of her being a young mom with a family of her own was not a factor. Because Lana would occasionally take Jason out of the hospital and go places, Jason looked forward to her coming. Sometimes she would take him to the movies, and sometimes she would just drive through McDonalds and get him whatever he wanted. Lana was outgoing and fun to be around. They developed a very special relationship.

Jason had been selected to plug in the Christmas tree for the City of Vancouver for Christmas 1994. Lana took him to the building where the Christmas tree had been prepared, and as they waited to enter the elevator to go to the building's roof, Anne Murray, an icon in Canadian music, walked out of the same elevator. Lana immediately recognized her, and as they passed by each other, blurted out, "Hi, Anne Murray!" Later she said, "Oh, I can't believe I just called her Anne Murray!" Jason got a big laugh out of the situation.

Lana's special relationship with Jason meant so much to us. When we left Jason in Lana's care, we could relax in our time off with the full knowledge that Jason loved being with Lana. She was a real blessing to all of us.

Trevor

JASON LOVED HOCKEY. Because of his illness, he never played organized hockey, although he would play goalie on the rug at home. Jason's love of the game led to some special relationships with people he considered to be superstars.

Trevor Linden of the Vancouver Canucks was one of these very special persons. Trevor made it a habit to visit kids at Children's Hospital. He would casually ask what kinds of things they liked to play with. We noticed that Trevor was usually accompanied by a young woman, who stood discretely off to the side and appeared to keep notes of these conversations. It was apparent that Trevor wanted to be certain that he never missed following up on anything that he promised to one of these kids.

On one particular follow-up visit, Trevor came into Jason's room and said, "Jason, you just wouldn't guess what I found lying out in the parking lot on my way up to see you." He handed Jason a brand-new Nintendo game, still in the box. He went on, "Could you imagine that? That somebody would just leave something like this? I saw it there, and then I thought, 'Hey, this is exactly what Jason was looking for!' So I said to myself, 'Isn't that amazing!'"

Trevor was such a humble guy—he would never say, "I went out and bought this for you." Later, after Trevor had left, we stepped out into the hall and noticed the empty shopping bag with the sales receipt still inside, discarded in the trash can.

On another occasion, we had tickets to see the Vancouver Grizzlies basketball game. Trevor had earlier told Jason that he was going to be at that same game and promised that he would be looking out for him. We didn't see Trevor that night, but he apparently saw Jason. A short time later, Trevor visited the hospital again and mentioned that he saw us and noticed Jason trying unsuccessfully to catch one of the T-shirts the cheerleaders shot into the stands with an air cannon. He said, "I happen to know the Griz [mascot of the Grizzlies] personally, so I went down to see him. Look what he gave me!" He handed Jason one of the T-shirts.

Just before Christmas in 1995, Jason was released from the hospital and allowed to come home. One of Scott's friends was over visiting, and as we were eating supper together, the phone rang. I answered the phone and heard the voice on the other end say, "Hello. Is this Mr. Anderson?" I said it was, so the speaker continued, "This is Trevor Linden. You're Jason's dad, right? Would it be all right with you if I spoke to Jason?"

I said, "Sure!" I turned and said to Jason, "Trevor Linden is on the phone."

Jason talked to him like he was an old buddy. As he talked, Scott became very excited. His friend did not believe that Trevor Linden was talking to Jason. He was shaking his head—no way. At that point in the conversation Trevor asked Jason if there was anything he could do for him right now.

Jason grinned. "Yeah. Could you talk to my neighbor? He doesn't believe that it's really you."

Trevor responded, "Put him on."

Jason handed the phone to Scott's friend, and as we watched, his jaw dropped. About all he could do was respond, "Uh-huh. Uh-huh." After a few minutes, he handed the phone back to Jason, dumbfounded. Jason became known around Moricetown as the friend of Trevor Linden, and for Jason, that was supremely cool.

Dave, Geoff, and Steve

THERE WERE A NUMBER OF SPECIAL Canucks besides Trevor Linden. Dave Babych was a real friendly guy, as was Geoff Courtnall. They were such an encouragement to all of us. Early on, when Jason had just started his treatments and his hair had just fallen out, we were able to go to a Canucks game. As we were settling into our seats, someone sat down in our nearly vacant row. It turned out to be Geoff Courtnall.

Just before one of the period intermissions, Geoff scooted closer to me. "Is this boy on the other side of you your son?" When I said he was, Geoff continued, "Does he have what I think he has?" I said yes. He paused for a moment. "OK. Would you mind if I gave him a present?" I said that would be fine.

Geoff disappeared, and when the third period began, he came back, sat beside me, and handed Jason one of his hockey sticks. He said, "Jason, my name is Geoff Courtnall. I signed this for you. I want you to have this."

Jason's face lit up. "Oh, I know who you are."

I thanked Geoff for what he had just done for Jason.

He shrugged. "Oh, it's nothing. I don't mind."

After the game, as we were walking down the hall, a kid came up and asked where Jason got the stick. Jason said, "That is Geoff Courtnall's stick. He gave it to me."

The kid looked at me and said, "Gee, I wish I could be your son."

You don't know what you are saying. You don't know what it cost Jason to get that stick.

On another occasion, the Canucks had only two tickets available for a certain special game. Scott and Jason both wanted to go, but we were one ticket short. I phoned Steve Tambellini, who worked in the front office.

"I have only two tickets. I'm OK with them being there, as long as somebody from the Canucks could meet these boys at the door and Jason could sit with Scott. I want them both to go, and I'll wait for them in the parking lot."

Steve said that would be fine and that he would make sure someone helped us with that.

Just before game time, I went to the gate Steve had told us to report to. A friendly lady met us and escorted us up to where the two seats were. She said I could stay with the boys before the game started—just to be sure they were all settled. As I was doing that, Steve showed up. He asked if we were doing OK, and I said we were. He looked at Jason sitting there and said to me, "You know, that seat is so low. Your son will have a really hard time seeing if he's sitting down in that seat, down so low. I'll bet that if he's on your lap, he could see a lot better. Don't you think so?"

I said, "Yeah, maybe."

Steve said, "Why don't you do that?"

So we all got to stay. We used only the two seats, and I held Jason on my lap. He was only eight years old at the time, so he wasn't very heavy. We appreciated what Steve did for us that day. We deeply appreciated these special things that so many people did for us. Even though we were going through difficult times, we were able to enjoy a number of memorable, special times.

Jason and a friend (also fighting cancer) enjoying a Vancouver Canucks game from the VIP box.

Kenny and Victor

THE NEXT ROUNDS OF CHEMOTHERAPY were as devastating to Jason as the first ones had been. He couldn't eat anything and keep it down. Surprisingly, though, when he regained the first hint of appetite, he wanted smoked half-dried salmon from Moricetown, prepared the traditional Wet'suwet'en way. Because his immune system was compromised, we couldn't just get it from the smokehouse. It had to be processed to commercial standards.

Kenny, a friend and neighbor in Moricetown, heard about Jason's craving and immediately arranged for the delivery of specially packaged salmon that was safe for Jason to eat. Jason wouldn't eat much, but he did begin to eat. For that reason, we always kept some of Kenny's half-dry salmon on hand. We later found out that he had organized fish fries at the Moricetown Canyon to raise money to help us. Another friend and neighbor, Warner, was also involved in this practical help to us.

We were sustained by the support we received from people in Moricetown. Although it was a fourteen-hour drive from Moricetown to Vancouver, we had many visitors from home. One of these was Victor Jim, Jason's former school principal. Victor came by Jason's hospital room and was upbeat, making Jason laugh. After a great visit, he excused himself and left. I wanted to privately thank him for coming, so I followed him out into the hall. I caught up to Victor as he was waiting at the elevator, and as I approached, I could see that he was weeping. All during the visit, he hadn't given a hint of how he felt. Seeing Victor standing there meant a lot to me. I gave him a big hug and told him how much I appreciated his coming. He said it was the least he could do. I don't think he understood how much of an encouragement he was to Jason and me that day, and would be to me in the days to come.

The Lund

DURING THE SUMMER OF 1994, the Make-a-Wish Foundation approached us and asked Jason to give some thought about something he really wanted to have. Right away, he responded that he wanted a quad. At the time we had a Honda minibike, which Jason had greatly enjoyed. He thought a quad would be more stable, which would be better for him. He was told that Make-a-Wish Foundation would not grant any motorized vehicles, so to ask for something else.

Because Jason loved to fish, he began talking about wanting to go on a guided fishing trip. I told him I would continue to take him fishing—perhaps he should ask for something else. Jason thought for a while. "How about a boat? Then I could go fishing in the boat." The Make-a-Wish Foundation gave Jason a fourteen-foot Lund on a trailer, delivered to our house in Surrey. Many people had generously contributed money to help us with the added expenses, so we had funds to get an outboard motor and steering system. Jason quickly learned to operate the boat, and the steering system made it possible for him to drive the boat when the conditions were suitable.

In the months ahead, whenever Jason got well enough to get out of the hospital between rounds of chemo, we were out on the water enjoying that boat. Sometimes we went boating on local lakes, such as at Golden Ears Provincial Park, but most of the time we took that small boat out into the ocean, usually fishing for little sand sharks and catching baby octopuses. The prospect of going out in the boat helped to give Jason the desire to get up from the hospital bed. We deeply appreciate the Make-a-Wish Foundation for making this possible.

We used that boat many, many times. We had great adventures in English Bay and around Burrard Inlet, making numerous fishing

Escaping in the Lund

expeditions. Despite occasional scares, even being caught in riptides, this boat enabled us to do things as a family that we wouldn't have been able to do otherwise, and most important, Jason was able to do what he loved to do—go fishing. If Jason was well enough to be released from the hospital, we went out in the Lund. The Lund was our oasis during his chemotherapy.

Home Again

IT TOOK SIXTEEN MONTHS to complete the regimen of chemotherapy. In November 1994, the cancer appeared to be eradicated. We could go home to Moricetown, though Jason would need to return to Vancouver for monitoring every three months initially. The plan was to increase the time between checkups to every six months, then to once a year. Hopefully, if the cancer remained in remission for five years, Jason could be pronounced cured.

That was a happy November day. We made arrangements to fly home, and when we arrived back at the Smithers Airport, we were greeted by a mob of well-wishers. The small arrivals area was packed with people displaying banners, streamers, and balloons. Sherrie and I had been home several times for short visits, but this marked the first time that Jason had returned to Moricetown since he went to Vancouver sixteen months before. A number of the crowd were from Jason's Christian school, and many others were from churches in Smithers. Many people present were from Moricetown. This unexpectedly extravagant welcome was a special time for us all.

Soon afterward, Jason started going back to school again, and life began to return to normal. We were so glad to be back in Moricetown again. Jason continued to take many medications in an effort to build his body back up and recover from the damage done by the chemotherapy. The following summer, in 1995, we made a deputation trip to the Midwest to visit our supporting churches. That trip was a great time of visitation, with many people eager to see Jason, who had been the object of their prayers. We rejoiced as a family the whole time.

We were beginning to put everything behind us. We knew it was possible the cancer could come back, but the doctors had told us they didn't expect it would. They felt the chemotherapy had given a good result, and we should be very hopeful. We were.

We were glad we had the Honda 50 minibike I had bought for Scott years before. Because Jason had been so weakened by the cancer treatments, he didn't have the strength to walk around the neighborhood. Consequently, he practically lived on that minibike. He loved the freedom it gave him to visit people in Moricetown. On more than one occasion, as Jason rode and I walked alongside him, he remarked that he didn't want ever to live anyplace other than Moricetown. He loved Moricetown. He was home again.

Homecoming in the Smithers Airport. November 1994.

Fear of the Known

IN APRIL 1996, Jason's arm became swollen. The puffiness and soreness concerned us. Jason was scheduled for a routine checkup near this time, and as Sherrie and I alternated taking him back to Vancouver for these checkups, Sherrie prepared for the trip. Just before they flew down, Sherrie shared with me that the Lord had impressed Psalm 112 on her that morning. She had been wondering what the Lord was saying to her. When I read that psalm, I did not like what I read.

> Praise the LORD.
> Blessed are those who fear the LORD,
> who find great delight in his commands.
> Their children will be mighty in the land;
> the generation of the upright will be blessed.
> Wealth and riches are in their houses,
> and their righteousness endures forever.
> Even in darkness light dawns for the upright, for those who
>   are gracious and compassionate and righteous.
> Good will come to those who are generous and lend freely,
> who conduct their affairs with justice.
> Surely the righteous will never be shaken;
> they will be remembered forever.
> They will have no fear of bad news;
> their hearts are steadfast, trusting in the LORD.
> Their hearts are secure, they will have no fear;
> in the end they will look in triumph on their foes.

As I read, fear came through me again. *Is the Lord getting us ready for something? What's going on?*

As planned, Sherrie took Jason down to Vancouver for his checkup, and I stayed home with Scott and Matthew. I expected Sherrie to call me with the results, so I stayed near the telephone. When the call arrived, Scott and Matthew happened to be over at my parents' home in Smithers, and I was alone in my office. I picked up the phone, fully expecting Sherrie to be speaking on the other end. Instead of Sherrie, it was Jason's doctor.

She told me that Sherrie was sitting right beside her as she spoke, but that Sherrie had wanted her to call and speak to me because she didn't know what to say. Jason's doctor explained that it looked like Jason's cancer was back. More testing would be needed to determine whether the cancer was back, and she advised me to come to Vancouver right away. We were going to have to make some big decisions that had to do with quality of life and what we should do and how we should move forward. It was very clear to me. *This isn't good.*

I could feel my whole body sliding into shock. Then Sherrie came on the line, crying. We talked a short while and then prayed briefly. I hung up the phone, devastated, and cried as I walked through our house.

When we had gone down to Vancouver the first time, I was afraid of the unknown. Now I feared the known. I knew we didn't want this cancer to come back. I knew this was worse than the first time.

Silence

BECAUSE HOSPITAL STAFF HAD SAID that Sherrie and I probably needed to be alone as we faced these decisions, I made arrangements for Matthew and Scott to stay with my parents. I was on the next available flight to Vancouver. Shortly after my arrival, we met with the team of doctors, who explained to us the tests that would be performed and what the tests would indicate. We had several difficult days waiting for the test results to be returned.

We checked into Ronald McDonald house again. Once there, we saw that another couple that we had gotten to know before was also back at Children's Hospital. Their daughter Julie had battled leukemia since she was five years old. A bone marrow transplant done previously had been successful, and she had been sent home with a positive prognosis. Now she was back, and her parents had just learned that this time the prognosis was that she was terminal. As we visited together, they sympathized with us. We had a common bond, although we did not know the final prognosis for Jason.

Those were dark, dark days. It seemed like heaven was glassed over, and I had a hard time praying. The morning we were to meet with the doctors and hear the results of the tests, I jogged down to Capilano Beach. At the end of the beach were some big rocks. I climbed out over the water on these rocks, and as I sat down, I thought of Psalm 112:

> Surely the righteous will never be shaken;
> they will be remembered forever.
> They will have no fear of bad news;
> their hearts are steadfast, trusting in the LORD.

I told the Lord, "I must not be a very righteous man, because I am terrified of bad news. I don't want to be terrified, but I am. I can't sense Your
presence. Everything seems so dark, and I can't tell that You are even
here. I hate where I am. I want to know You are here, but I can't feel You."
As I sat there on the rocks, there was just silence. It seemed like
God was not answering me. I had no comfort or sense of His presence. I
even cried out that feeling to the Lord. As I began jogging back, for some
reason my thoughts turned to Proverbs 21:31. To paraphrase that verse,
a man prepares his horse for the battle, but the battle belongs to the
Lord. I thought of 2 Chronicles 20:15, where God tells Israel through the
prophet Jahaziel, "This is what the LORD says to you: 'Do not be afraid or
discouraged because of this vast army. For the battle is not yours, but
God's'". I thought of other passages throughout the Old Testament that
said that armies would equip themselves to fight, but God was the one
who gave them victory. The people were to lean on God, not on their
weapons, not on their horses. I wasn't sure why, but I continued thinking about these passages while I was running back.

A few hours later, I understood. God was preparing me for a difficult
conversation.

Peace

SHERRIE AND I WENT ALONE to the hospital. Earlier the doctors had asked us not to bring Jason to this meeting. That in itself scared us; up to that point, Jason had been invited. We met the team of doctors in the outpatient area of the cancer ward.

I hated and feared that place. The very first time I went in there, it was one of the most terrifying places I had been in my life. We walked in with an apparently healthy boy, and we found ourselves surrounded by people hooked up to IV needles, some with no hair, some skin and bones, some overweight, some getting blood, but all there because of cancer. We got used to the sights and sounds eventually, but now we were terrified in a different way.

The doctors walked toward us like executioners.

They asked us to come into a meeting room. We knew that many, many people were praying for us. As we walked into that room, I had one of the strangest experiences in my life. A profound peace came over both Sherrie and me—a peace that we could not understand. The doctors sat down, and we engaged in the obligatory small talk before getting down to business. We were told that the tests were conclusive—the cancer had returned both to Jason's arm and to his lungs, and possibly spread to other places as well. We were told that this team of doctors had never had a child patient in whom Ewing's sarcoma had returned and the child had survived. One doctor flatly stated, "We are telling you today, Jason is not going to survive. He's going to die."

As I listened, I felt an incomprehensible calmness. I wasn't sad; I was utterly calm. "OK, what are our options, and what are we looking at here?"

One of the doctors repeated, "We want you to understand. Whatever we tell you from this point forward, Jason is going to die. He is not going to make it. We have some things to try, but they aren't going to give you any hope that he will survive. Do you understand that?"

Together we said, "Yes, we do."

Two of the doctors who were closest to Jason said, "You don't seem like you understand it." They looked at each other and said again, "You don't seem like you understand it."

"No, we understand. Before you came into this room, and before Jason ever had cancer, he was in God's hands. Now, when you come in and tell us this, nothing has changed. He is still in God's hands."

Their expressions remained doubtful. "It's good you can have that kind of faith. You hang on to that. You'll need it."

I felt a deep calmness of heart. "We are convinced that is the way it is. We just need to know what we need to do now."

The team of doctors began to outline a difficult, experimental program of treatment. Throughout the explanation, we got the clear impression that, although there was no hope for a cure, Jason's participation would help them learn things that might lead to future breakthroughs. I asked the doctors how much time Jason had left.

"If we don't pursue any further treatment, likely a couple of months at best."

Neither option was good.

We discussed how we were going to tell this news to Jason. We decided we would talk to him alone, and afterward meet with the doctors again to make quality-of-life decisions. Jason had not handled chemotherapy well the first time; this would be even worse.

Sherrie and I left and went outside the hospital to our vehicle. At first we sat talking about how we should go about telling our ten-year-old child he was going to die. We initially thought we should drive around Stanley Park and discuss it further. I actually started the vehicle, but we both concluded that this conversation would never get easier. I switched off the ignition, and we prayed, thanking God and asking Him to help us tell Jason. Then we drove directly back to Ronald McDonald House, where Jason waited.

We Can Still Go Out to Supper, Can't We?

BEFORE THE MEETING WITH THE DOCTORS, we had made plans to go out for supper that night with our friend Julie and her parents. At this point, though, dinner plans were the furthest thing from our minds. When we arrived at Ronald McDonald House, we found Jason in the TV room and asked him to come upstairs where we could talk privately. As we walked upstairs, I was torn. My mind refused to believe this was actually happening, yet I knew it really was.

We had been given the extra-big room at Ronald McDonald House. We had long ago discovered that they give you the extra-big, nice room when you have bad things to deal with. We would so much have preferred to be crammed into a corner somewhere rather than be given this grand room. Once inside, I sat on the daybed and took Jason into my lap and held him. I knew I had to tell him, but I still had no good plan. After a few moments, I just began.

"Jason, we just talked to the doctors. They said that your cancer has returned and that they don't believe that they can cure you."

Jason leaned his head against my chest and sobbed. Sherrie and I sat close together and held on to Jason as we all cried together. After what seemed like just a few seconds, Jason suddenly stopped and looked up at me. He gave me a big hug.

"It's OK, Dad. I'll just be in heaven," he said matter-of-factly, as if he were saying he would be in the next room.

I was so proud of Jason and so grateful to God that He had enabled Jason to say what he had just said. It was so good to hear his expression of confidence in God. At the same time, I hated to hear him speak that way. *You're not supposed to go there before me. That's not the way it's supposed to be!* I didn't give voice to any of those thoughts; we held on to each other as Sherrie and I continued to weep. When our crying subsided, Jason asked, "We can still go out to supper with Julie, can't we?"

I couldn't believe what I heard. Jason saw his situation so clearly. His conviction that he would be in heaven allowed him to be at peace in what was, through his faith, an absolute certainty. "Of course, we can go out to supper with Julie," I replied.

But before supper we had a choice to make—we could go home and let the cancer run its course, or we could do some treatments that might help. These treatments would be difficult.

"I'm not going back into the hospital," Jason blurted. "Let's just go home."

I didn't want to do that—I wasn't ready to give up. Yet, Jason was ten and a half years old, and he needed to be involved in this decision. It was his life.

We told him we understood that he was the one who was going to go through it. I told him about the verses I had been thinking about while jogging that morning. God had promised victory to Israel, but He still expected them to pick up their swords, their spears, and their shields and to go into battle. As they went into battle, they weren't supposed to trust in those weapons but in God for the outcome. Right now, the only sword or spear we had to carry into battle was chemotherapy. Maybe we should pick it up and trust the Lord, and use the weapons we have.

Jason processed that. "OK."

With the decision made, we went out and enjoyed a great evening with Julie and her parents. Julie's leukemia had been pronounced terminal only a few days before, so of all people on earth, they understood.

Waterfalls, Squirrels, and Something Worse than Cancer

WE IMMEDIATELY WENT BACK to Moricetown with Jason to prepare to move again to Vancouver. We broke the news to Matthew and Scott and began to make plans. The first thing we did was to take some private family time. We packed up our tent and camping gear and drove to a special place in the bush not far from our house and set up camp near a waterfall.

The following morning was a Sunday, so we had our own family Sunday service around the campfire. We prayed together about what was coming and then spent the rest of the day hiking and playing and enjoying being together as a family. In the first sixteen months that we had been in Vancouver, we had learned that if there is an opportunity to have fun, you take advantage of it. You don't think about tomorrow, but you enjoy the day. Otherwise, you will lose the opportunity that presents itself today.

We had a great time together, and in the course of our time in the bush, finalized decisions that had to be made. This time, we would not move into a house in Vancouver; Sherrie and I would stay at Ronald McDonald House while Jason was having treatments. Scott and Matthew would stay in Smithers with their grandparents and continue to attend their regular school. Initially, Sherrie and I would both go to Vancouver with Jason; later we would alternate, with one remaining in Vancouver while the other stayed home with Scott and Matthew. With the great distances involved, it was incredibly challenging to maintain a semblance of normal family life.

When we first arrived back in Vancouver, we took advantage of our last opportunity to have fun. We went to Stanley Park, Jason's favorite place in Vancouver, and watched him chasing squirrels. It seemed like he wanted to get in all the running he could, because he knew he wasn't going to be able to run once his treatments began. The following day, chemotherapy treatments started again, and we soon discovered that the doctors had not understated their warning: these experimental treatments were brutally difficult. Despite the passage of time, Jason's body was still weakened from the initial sixteen months of chemotherapy. This time, it was much worse. His adverse reactions, including constant vomiting, returned with a vengeance.

There were occasional bright moments. Mattel Corporation sent a representative, the official Barbie, to Children's Hospital. Barbie visited the children confined there and distributed Mattel toys. Naturally, all of the girls were excited, but Jason consented to meet with Barbie only because he was interested in other toys she might have. To his mortification, Barbie chose to have promotional pictures taken featuring her and Jason, pictures that eventually were distributed widely about the province in newspapers and other media. To him, having his picture with Barbie was the worst thing that had happened to him that year—including the news that his cancer had returned.

It Isn't Always What You Think You See

ONCE AGAIN, DEATH SURROUNDED US. A few rooms down from Jason's, a thirteen-year-old boy was dying. Although his mother had shared this information with us, for some reason she had chosen not to tell her son that he had only a few weeks left. Somehow, when his mother left the hospital for a short time, word got to him. He came storming into Jason's room and declared, "Well, in a couple of weeks I'll be pushing up daisies." He talked it over at length with Jason. Situations like this were not uncommon.

Another time, I was in the room with Jason when we heard loud wailing in the hall. I went outside the room and saw a man we knew well. This man's daughter had leukemia. I went out to him and learned that his daughter had just died on the operating table. I held him as we stood in the hallway. There was nothing I could say, but I felt his pain because my son faced the same prognosis. This grief-stricken father had known this awful day would come but hadn't thought it would come so quickly. As I looked over his shoulder, I could see the floor nurses signaling to me to move him, if at all possible, from the hallway and into a room. They wanted to respect his grief, but they were concerned for all of the other parents of desperately sick children. I was able to get him into a side room, where he continued to sob. I have a special bond with this man to this day.

Those were difficult days. Death was always near. During this time, we attended the funeral of Andrew, Power Ranger Billy. We watched as both disease and the harsh treatments intended to combat disease devastated the children around us. One of these was Jason's roommate,

Mark, another of Trevor Linden's boys. Mark and our son Matthew had grown close to each other. He was a pleasant boy, but as chemotherapy debilitated his body, his personality sometimes became demanding and mean.

We had a visitor who commented to me that Mark was a very spoiled kid. Mark couldn't have overheard it, but I nonetheless took our visitor out of the room. "Oh, don't ever say that about him. He is not a spoiled little kid. When he came in here, he was the nicest kid you would ever want to meet. He was polite. His body has been ravaged by cancer and these drugs. You've got to be gracious here. It isn't always what you see, or what you think you see."

It is so natural to make judgments based on what we see, yet without having the full picture. Our visitor that day had reached conclusions that were not fair, much as I had done several years before at Ronald McDonald House when I thought a child was receiving unwarranted special treatment. Compassion demands that we look deeper.

Apathy

I HAD GREAT PEACE as we headed into chemotherapy again; paradoxically, I became distant in my relationship with the Lord. I began to struggle with apathy and depression. When I was honest with myself, what scared me most about this was that I didn't care that I wasn't doing well with the Lord. James 5 admonishes us to confess our faults to one another. For the first time in my life as a Christian, I had no desire to acknowledge my faults to myself, much less anyone else. I simply didn't care.

After our initial time with Jason in Vancouver, Sherrie and I alternated between staying with Jason in the hospital and coming back to Moricetown to stay with Scott and Matthew as we had planned. Occasionally, Jason would be released from the hospital, and Sherrie or I would stay with him at Ronald McDonald House. Even less frequently, Sherrie or I would just stay at Ronald McDonald House alone for a break.

Several times on these rare breaks, I watched some things on TV that I normally never would have watched—at least not without my conscience giving me a difficult time. Before, I would say, "I've got to get away from this stuff!"

I don't care about trying to walk away from this. I don't care. I'm sitting here, and I'm not going to walk away. I felt guilty, but I didn't care that I felt guilty. I sensed that I was in a very dangerous place. I felt like God was distant and wasn't answering us. Part of me knew that wasn't true, but I continued to think this way.

Things came to a head the next time I went back to Moricetown while Sherrie stayed in Vancouver with Jason. I had been reading the book of Job, and I asked the Lord to help me. "Lord, I know I'm in trouble. I'm in really deep trouble, and I don't know what to do." I was challenged by Job 31:10–12, where Job said in effect, "If I have looked upon a woman in a lustful way, I deserve to be condemned." *I'm guilty of that.* I admitted my guilt to God as I drove through Smithers. "Lord, could You send someone to help me! I need help, and I don't know what to do. I'm not going to search somebody out, but I need help."

I came to a stoplight. As I looked ahead, I noticed an old friend of mine on the other side of the intersection. As we passed, he motioned to me that we should go for a coffee. In all the years I have known him, that is the only time we have ever gone for coffee. When we sat down, I told him about my spiritual apathy and the clear sense that things were wrong in my life.

He said, "Doug, I wouldn't feel that way. I think that if there is stuff wrong in your life, God will clearly show you what it is."

I kind of smiled at him. "But he did."

My friend retorted, "Oh!"

"I need you to pray for me. I just need you to pray for me."

He said he would, and that encouraged me a little. God was beginning to rescue me from myself, and He was using people to do it.

Pastor Don

WHILE I WAS IN TOWN that day, I had planned to leave some promotional brochures with several pastors. One of the churches I stopped at had taken a great interest in praying for Jason. I went into the church office to drop off the brochure with the secretary and noticed the door to the pastor's study was open. As I handed the secretary the brochure, she asked if I needed to talk to the pastor. I said, "No, just give him this."

As I turned to walk out, Pastor Don heard my voice and called out, "Doug, is that you?" When I answered, he said, "Have you got a minute?"

More from a sense of obligation than anything else, I responded, "Sure!" I walked into his office.

"Shut the door and have a seat." When I did, he asked, "Doug, how are you doing?"

A floodgate opened, and I fell apart right there in that chair. I had no idea any of this was coming. I wept uncontrollably. I hadn't cried like that since Jason was diagnosed with cancer. Everything I was feeling poured out. I couldn't have chosen a better guy with whom to have that happen than this humble, gentle pastor the Lord had brought me to that day. He wept with me, and when I shared with him that I didn't care anymore, he wept with me about that. Then he shared with me the struggles within his church and how he'd gotten so depressed he felt like quitting. We wept together again. Then we prayed for each other.

This was a turning point in my life. God was picking me up again, and He was using unlikely people to do it. God continued to do this through John, Daren, and many others. I could see how He was using people in my life, and as a by-product, I began to see how men in our church were growing in the Lord. Individuals said I was discipling them. *How can I be discipling you? I'm hardly even making it myself!*

I understood then that I had a shallow, insufficient view of what discipleship is. While there is nothing wrong with going through books or having Bible studies together, discipleship is far more than that. Discipleship is showing someone how to walk with the Lord—and you cannot show someone how to do something that you can't do yourself. Sherrie and I had been hanging on by the skin of our teeth, unaware that people were observing our struggle. I began to appreciate these men deeply, because I saw how much I needed them. As far as I was concerned, I wasn't building them up—they were upholding me. I began to realize that discipleship is more than just teaching; it is coming into deep relationship with people as we experience God together.

Through my experience with Jason, God was doing deep things in me. He was working in my inmost person, my very heart. In the process, my relationship with Him and the idea that His mercies are new every morning came to me so sweet and so fresh. It was transforming to know God was saying, "Doug, you know things haven't changed between Me and you. You can trust Me in this."

Jason was very sick, and life was hard, but his faith in the Lord didn't waver. He trusted the Lord and was actually doing well. Like Jason, I began to trust the Lord in deeper, more profound ways.

Yahoo!

JASON WAS IN THE EXPERIMENTAL treatment program for nine months. We hoped the treatment would allow a successful bone marrow transplant. The idea was to harvest Jason's bone marrow, give him a dose of chemotherapy that would devastate the cancer cells (while wiping out his bone marrow), and then reintroduce Jason's own bone marrow. The anticipated chemotherapy was so heavy and severe, there was a great risk that Jason would die from the treatment itself. The risk of the proposed procedure was justified only by the fact that Jason was already dying.

We were faced with another difficult decision. Sherrie and I both felt in our hearts that this procedure would be fatal to Jason. Yet up to that point, we had always followed the doctor's advice, and we determined that we would continue to do so. Because we were so conflicted, we spent much time praying for wisdom.

The day before the proposed bone marrow transplant, Jason, Sherrie, and I went to the hospital for consultation with the medical team. As we were preparing to sit down in the consultation room, we were asked to have Jason wait outside while the team met with Sherrie and me. This was not usual. Still not understanding, Sherrie and I went into the meeting.

The room was filled with people. One of the team explained they had been monitoring the growth in Jason's lungs but had somehow failed to compare the most recent images with the original image. When the proper comparison was made, they discovered that despite the intense chemotherapy to date, the cancer in Jason's lungs had continued to grow. It was the opinion of the medical team that to proceed with the bone marrow transplant and more chemotherapy would likely kill Jason outright and have little effect in slowing the cancer. In the interest of Jason's quality of life, the team recommended that the bone marrow transplant not be done, and that the experimental chemotherapy be stopped.

Sherrie and I were almost happy. This puzzled the medical team. We told them we had been praying about this decision and had asked God to show us clearly whether we should proceed. Their advice seemed pretty clear—we should stop treatment and go home. We discussed things further for a few minutes, and then the doctors asked us if we wanted to tell Jason or if we wanted them to tell him. We agreed that they should give him the news.

The doctor who was to tell Jason said, "If Jason asks, 'Am I going to die?' I am going to tell him yes. Are you OK with that?" Sherrie and I affirmed that we were.

Jason was called in, and the doctor explained everything to him. Despite being fully aware of what this meant, when told that he could go home, Jason exclaimed, "Yahoo!"

"Is there anything we can do for you?" the doctor asked.

Jason pointed to the port in his chest. "Can you take this out today?"

Fully aware of the logistical issues of getting this done on such short notice, the doctors looked at each other. The doctor who was speaking for the team said, "Jason, I am going to work on that one. I will pull every string I can pull. If it's possible, it will happen today."

It was possible. The port was removed just a few hours later.

I Think this Message Is for You

JASON WAS RELEASED from the hospital that night. We were told he might live weeks, maybe months, but not years. Before heading home the following morning, we decided to drive out to Chilliwack to attend a prayer meeting.

A sister mission was conducting a prayer retreat at a park on Cultus Lake. Along with others from that mission, my dad was present. Anticipating the bone marrow reintroduction, we had asked if we could come so they could lay hands on Jason and pray for him. When we finally arrived, the meeting was well underway. Sherrie and I and Jason sat in the back row and joined the seventy others who were already in session.

The speaker was a man I had never met. As he spoke, I glanced at my watch and took note of the time. Jason had promised a friend in Moricetown that he would call him that night, so I leaned over and whispered to Sherrie, "There's a phone booth outside—you can call from there." Sherrie and Jason quietly got up and slipped out of the meeting.

At exactly that moment the speaker began to tell the story of his wife, who died of cancer. Her cancer debilitated her so much that she had to be fed. Because the cancer had spread to her brain, she lost her ability to communicate. Near the end, a pastor happened to visit and asked our speaker if he could pray with his wife. The speaker said that he could, but that she was not capable of communicating or even of knowing that he was praying. Not dissuaded, the pastor prayed with her anyway. As he left, he slipped a piece of paper into our speaker's hand.

When alone, our speaker opened the paper and read the message. "I have asked God to give you and your wife one more time that you can talk together."

Our speaker said, "That is ridiculous. Why would God do that? If God can make her able to talk to me again, why doesn't he just heal her? Why would God do that?" In disgust, he crumpled the note and threw it into the wastebasket.

That night, as he was feeding his wife with an eyedropper, she suddenly said in a clear voice, "This is my favorite time of night."

Our speaker replied, "What do you mean?"

"This is the time of night when you and I can talk together." She asked him to go get a piece of paper and a pencil, and she continued, "I want you to write down the names of people I want to thank for helping you through this time." She dictated a list of names, and he wrote them down. When he got to the end of the list, she said, "Last of all, I want to thank you for all that you have been doing and for how you love me." As they conversed, the last intelligible thing she said was how she appreciated that he always remembered to look both ways before he crossed a street. Then she slipped back into unconsciousness and died several days later.

The speaker concluded by saying that God was not just the God of the mountains but also the God of the valley. I Kings 20:23 records that after the Israelites had defeated their enemies in the mountains, the defeated king said, "Their gods are gods of the hills. That is why they were too strong for us. But if we fight them on the plains, surely we will be stronger than they". The speaker's message to us was that God is also the God of the valley, and He wins victories in the valleys too. He testified that God had won a victory in his life and taught him that God was taking his wife home—not because His hand was too short to save her, but because He had a plan, He had a purpose. God's allowing her to talk that night displayed this clearly.

After he finished speaking, as others were singing and finishing the service, he walked straight back without a word to anyone and sat down beside me.

"You must be Jason's dad," he said.

I said I was.

"I have to say something to you. I believe with all my heart that God wanted me to bring this message tonight. I prayed about it a lot, but then you and Jason and your wife came into the room. I looked at him, with no hair, and I looked at my notes, explaining how my wife died from cancer, and I thought, no way am I going to share that. This young boy has cancer. I must have been wrong. I must have misunderstood, and it was not God. Right up until then, I had been so sure that it was God telling me to share this. Then, as I was speaking and going through my notes, just as I came to the spot where I was going to share the story, your boy and wife got up and left. So, I shared it." He leaned closer and reached out to me. "I think this message is for you."

In all honesty, I didn't want to hear that.

God Just Changes Everything

THE SERVICE CAME TO AN END, and Jason and Sherrie came back into the room. Someone called me up to the front, still expecting that we would have a time of prayer regarding the bone marrow transplant. Instead, I began to share how the doctors had concluded that the treatments would not work, and that they were sending us home. Treatment was done. I broke down as I said we still needed to pray.

Everybody in that place was crying. Someone called for Jason, Sherrie, and my dad to join me at the front. The whole group, seventy strong, gathered around us and prayed. It was a special, powerful time. We knew we were surrounded by wise men of God who were asking for what God wanted. Two things stood out—they were after what God wanted, and they cared deeply for us.

Except for Jason, everyone in the room was crying.

We left the meeting at around 11:00 p.m. It was pouring rain. As we walked out to our car, Jason said, "Dad, do you know why I wasn't crying?"

I said, "Well, you were the only one who wasn't crying. Why weren't you crying?"

"We think we know what's going to happen. We get all worried about what's going to happen, and then God just changes everything. So I'm not going to worry about it."

I said, "Jason, you know what? That is exactly how Jesus told us to think. He said don't take any thought for tomorrow. Today has enough worries of its own. You seek God in His kingdom, and He will take care of all the rest. Jason, you just keep thinking that way. You are right."

The Battle Belongs to the Lord

WE GOT INTO OUR CAR and started the long drive back to Ronald McDonald House, where we planned to spend the night before going back home to Moricetown the next day. It was late and pouring rain as we headed toward Vancouver on Highway 1. Sherrie and I were quietly talking in the front, and Jason was sitting in the backseat. Suddenly, Jason said, "Dad, turn up that song."

I said, "What song?"

Jason apparently thought I was teasing. "I mean the one on the stereo. You know. Turn it up."

"Jason, I don't have the radio or stereo on." And then I asked, "What song are you hearing?"

"You know, that song that says, 'We sing honor and power and glory to our God.' You know that song." Jason began reciting words as if he were repeating something he was listening to—the lyrics to "The Battle Belongs to the Lord." Sherrie and I couldn't hear it, but Jason was asking us to turn it up!

I said, "Do you hear that song?"

"Yeah!"

As we continued to drive, Jason settled back in the seat and slipped off into sleep. Sherrie and I drove in silence the rest of the way into Vancouver and back to Ronald McDonald House. The incident was powerful and moving. We are convinced that God gave this song to Jason to give to us. At that time, this song was quite new. While we had heard it occasionally on the radio, we had never actually sung it. Jason couldn't have known the lyrics by heart that night, but somehow God gave them to him. We were motivated to learn those lyrics ourselves, and they continue to minister powerfully to us to this day.

Life as Normal

THE FOLLOWING MORNING, we gathered our belongings from Ronald McDonald House and began the long drive to Moricetown. Jason wasn't feeling very sick and was thrilled to go home. He was bubbly, in fact. Even though he knew his was not a good report, he was so happy to be away from the hospital and all the cancer treatment.

We made a great effort as a family to try to get life back to normal as much as possible, and we largely succeeded. Because of the combined damage of the cancer and the treatments to fight the cancer, Jason was severely debilitated. Among other things, his kidneys were damaged, and he needed ongoing infusions of electrolytes. He regularly took sixty to seventy different pills each day. Despite that, we fell back into our regular routines. In the fall of 1997, Jason went back to school and rejoined his class and many friends.

One of the traditions we observe in our family is a special deer-hunting trip to Haida Gwaii to mark the boys' thirteenth birthdays. Even though Jason would not be thirteen until December, I took him early because we didn't know how long he would have relatively good health. While battling the cancer, I had often thought this was one trip we would never be able to make. I was so happy that we were able to go, and it turned out to be an amazing trip.

My dad, Jason, and I had a good ferry crossing from Prince Rupert, and almost immediately after we landed, we got several little bucks. Jason was delighted and in his element. He loved being outdoors and would sit quietly for long periods, studying everything around him.

I had acquired a .243 caliber rifle for Jason with a short stock that fit him. I installed a bipod on the fore end so he could shoot with one hand, since he was missing one of his shoulder joints. He could shoot with tremendous accuracy with that bipod. He was patient and skilled at spotting deer as they sneaked through the undergrowth. The second or third day out, Jason got two bucks the same day. Although he was cool and calm on the outside, you could tell that he was ecstatic.

The trip was a special, special time, made bittersweet with the knowledge that we would probably never do this again with him. We wanted to take it slow and appreciate every moment. I think we succeeded. Along with all the meat, we brought the hide from Jason's first deer home and had it tanned as a keepsake.

We made several other memorable trips. One was a visit to Edmonton. While we were there, the boys asked if I would call the Edmonton Oilers and see if they would give us tickets like the Canucks had done so often. I explained that the Oilers did not know us, and besides, Jason was not in treatment any longer. Scott and Jason persisted, so I agreed to try. I phoned the Oilers' office and explained our circumstances to the lady who answered the call. I ended by asking if it would be possible to get tickets to see the Oilers play that night. She asked me for my phone number and said she would call me back in a half an hour.

As promised, a half hour later, she called back and said she had five tickets waiting for us at the gate. I told her how much I appreciated that. "You don't even know if I'm telling the truth."

She replied, "Sir, I don't know of anybody who would lie about something like that." Later that evening, she met us at the gate and gave us the tickets. The Oilers treated us very well, and we treasure the memories of that evening when, as a family, we were able to watch the Oilers play.

Although he was very weak, Jason continued to live from day to day. The days became weeks, and the weeks became months. We were so grateful for that time and were grateful every moment.

Doug and Jason fishing for rainbow trout
on a lake near Moricetown.

What Is It Going to Take?

SHORTLY AFTER ABANDONING TREATMENTS and returning home, I made a trip to Fort St. James in my capacity as a field director. I met with several missionaries who lived and worked there, and one of them shared stories of past ministry in Fort St. James with me. Before I left, we had a good time of prayer out in his driveway, and as I prayed, I cried out to God for Tache, Binche, and surrounding First Nations reserves. As we prayed, I kept thinking to myself, "What is it going to take? What is it going to take, God?" In my heart I prayed, "Just do what You need to do to make a difference in those places?"

As we continued in prayer, I sensed that the Lord was saying to me, "Doug, even if it means taking your son home? Even if it means that?"

I didn't want to have that thought. I prayed, "Wow. What can I say to that? Lord, it is not my desire to see that, but I do want Your will to be done. I don't know how that would make any difference, but I just leave that with You."

I had several similar conversations with God. Another time, I was snowshoeing alone near our house. As I walked, I began to plead with God for the salvation of Jason's doctors—particularly our family doctor in Smithers. As I prayed, I again was strongly impressed that God was saying, "If that is what it took, would you be willing to give up your son for him?"

I fell down on my face in the snow. "Lord, what can I say? I have to say yes! You gave Your son for me—what else can I say? I have to say yes because of what You did. But that is not what I want to see happen."

Surprisingly, those were not terrifying conversations with God. I did not feel dread, but rather had special times with the Lord. I didn't see God as being mean to me. Instead, I felt His arms around me. I sensed that God was saying, "Doug, I want you to understand, I need you to understand, how much I love people. I want you to love people like I do."

Finish Saying It, Dad

THE FIRST FIFTEEN MONTHS after we came home from Vancouver flew by. We had many fun times together as a family, and for the most part, Jason was healthy. Just before April Fools' Day, Jason came home from school with an unusual request. He prefaced it by observing, "It doesn't matter what I do, I never get in trouble for it. I guess it's because I'm sick." Then he voiced the request: "Could I bring some stink bombs to school and throw them in places I'm not supposed to? I want to get into trouble."

It sounded funny. I said, "Sure. You go ahead." All on his own, Jason decided to throw one in the principal's car, among other places. Because of the blatant nature of what he had done, the principal felt compelled to call me. The phone call began, "Doug, I don't know what to do with this. I am really torn. I hate to call you about this, but I feel like I need to." He went on to explain what Jason had done.

I struggled to keep from laughing. "You know, Jason actually asked me if he could do that. He said he never gets in trouble and he wanted to, just once. Your phone call to me right now is the very thing Jason wants. He just wants to be a normal kid." We had a laugh together on the phone—a boy who asked his dad for permission to get into trouble.

Gradually, though, Jason developed more physical problems. In the spring of 1998, Sherrie went away to a ladies' retreat while I stayed with the boys at home. Jason was experiencing increasing problems with constipation due to some of the medication he was taking. Shortly after Sherrie left, he had such severe stomach cramps that I took him to the hospital emergency room at Smithers. Jason was screaming with pain, and I could not handle that. I called Sherrie to come back. I wanted her to have a good time with her friends, but it was so difficult to see him in such pain that I could not cope alone.

A few days after Sherrie returned, the hospital staff managed to get Jason's problem cleared up. But this marked the start of a down-hill slide. While Jason was in the hospital, they re-scanned his lung to assess the size of the tumor. We met with our doctor, who told us that the mass in Jason's lung was growing rapidly. We got the clear sense that the doctor was saying, "This is the end."

Although we'd known all along that things would come to this, this news swept over me like a terror. I had been thinking that maybe some-how we weren't going to have to deal with this. We were always holding out that the Lord could heal him. This news put me in shock once again.

We needed to have another talk with Jason and let him know what was going on.

To prepare for that, Sherrie and I went for a drive up Hudson's Bay Mountain. I stopped the car, and we got out at a place where we could see far off across the Bulkley Valley. We prayed together and gave the whole thing to the Lord. The Lord met us there. From the time we'd first heard the news, it seemed like I couldn't get my balance back, I couldn't get my feet under me. We sat and prayed, gazing out over God's creation, and there grew within me an increasing conviction that although this was incredibly frightening, we were not alone and were going to make it through this somehow. He was there with us.

We drove back down the mountain and went back to the hospital. I sat on the edge of Jason's bed, and as I tried to tell him that it looked like the tumor was growing fast in his chest, I stopped in the middle of my sentence. I couldn't speak. Despite my efforts not to, I began to cry. Jason held me in his arms and said over and over, "It's going to be OK, Dad. It's going to be OK. You can go ahead and finish saying it. It's OK. I'm OK. Finish saying it."

I somehow continued. "They think this is it, Jason. You are dying." There we sat, me crying and Jason holding me, telling me it was all right.

I am still astonished by the way the Lord worked in Jason's heart. I know he didn't like to see us crying, but his were not idle words designed to make us feel better. I saw an unshakable confidence in him—he really believed he was going to be OK, and we were all going to be OK.

The Fifth-Wheel Trailer

WHEN WE BROUGHT JASON HOME from the hospital, he declared that he didn't ever want to go back to the hospital again. Shortly afterward, his breathing became increasingly labored, and he began to struggle for every breath. We got an intercom system for the house so we could monitor him at night. It was a horrible time. Jason would lie on his back, and we would lie in our bed and listen to him gasping for air. Finally, I told Sherrie that I had to turn it off. The sound of his gasping for air tore me apart. It was incredibly difficult, but we shut the monitor off and prayed for him.

Jason began to fail quickly. At Matthew's birthday party, Jason could only watch as the other children played. As he deteriorated, one of his best friends, Vanya, became more and more important to him. He prayed for Vanya every night, often with tears, crying out to the Lord for his salvation. As Jason weakened, Vanya would come over as soon as he got out of school every day and sit with him until he had to go home and to bed. Often he would crawl up into bed with Jason just to be near him. He would come over on his days off school and spend the entire day with Jason. Jason got so he could talk in just whispers and was no longer able to breathe lying down. He could sleep only by leaning forward onto a pillow held in his lap.

We got an oxygen bottle, but Jason refused it. Sometimes when he fell asleep, I would try to slide the oxygen mask up by his nose, but he always pushed it away. It was almost like Jason was resigned to the fact—he was going to die, and he didn't want anything that would extend the process. Jason refused anything that smelled like or in any other way reminded him of the hospital. He told us a number of times that no matter what, he didn't want to go back to the hospital. We honored his wish.

Through all of this, his faith grew stronger. At one point, he called us all together and said to me, "We're not praying as a family anymore."

I said, "We're all still praying, but we haven't been praying together." I realized that Jason simply wanted us to pray together, as a family—not necessarily for his healing, but just to pray together. So we did.

As Jason grew weaker and weaker, I held on to the fact that God could heal him, and because He *could*, maybe He *would*. Near the end, we began to administer small doses of morphine. Eating became impossible for Jason. Surprisingly to us, as he continued to deteriorate, his hearing became hypersensitive. He soon could not tolerate conversation above a whisper, and routine household sounds became physically painful for him. He was able to hear things that even our dog apparently did not hear. Because of his sensitivity to sound, we moved him out of the house and set him up in my parents' fifth-wheel trailer. Someone stayed with him constantly.

Never Give Up

ON JUNE 3, Sherrie and I sat at the table in the fifth-wheel trailer having our devotions together. Jason was up on the bed behind us, sleeping in the sitting position. As we were reading our Bibles, we heard Jason whisper something. I couldn't make out what he'd said, so I asked Sherrie if she had understood him.

Sherrie replied, "I think he said, 'Don't give up.'"

We returned to our reading.

A short time later, we both heard Jason emphatically stage whisper, "Never give up!" I turned around and looked at him. He remained with his head down on his lap, sleeping. Sherrie and I looked at each other, wondering what that was all about.

We finished reading, and as we had planned to plant the garden that day, I carried Jason outside and put him in a lawn chair so he could watch Sherrie and me work. When we finished gardening, I carried Jason back to his bed in the trailer. As I carried him, I said, "Jason, it looked like you were sleeping this morning. You said, 'Don't give up.' Then later you said, 'Never give up.' I just wondered if you were sleeping. Do you remember what you were dreaming about?"

Jason gestured with his shoulder-less right arm, jabbing the air with his index finger for emphasis on each word. "No, I was not sleeping! You and Mom need to hear that."

I was speechless.

On a shelf in our living room we display a picture of Jason when he was four or five years old. Beside it is a plaque bearing Winston Churchill's famous quote: "Never, never, never give up." Jason was right— I needed to hear those words. A number of times since, his words have come back to me. When I have felt that things are too much and I can't deal with it anymore, I hear Jason's words ringing in my ears: "Never give up!"

I saw this same persistence in Jason regarding his faith in God. I know this persistence was not by Jason's own strength, but God was doing that in him. I am so grateful to God that he did that work in Jason. Jason's faith remained strong—not just surviving, but strong and thriving.

Someone's Tapping Me

THE NIGHT BEFORE JASON DIED, Sherrie was lying down with him in the trailer. In the early hours of the morning, I put a worship CD in the stereo and sat on the couch in our house, overwhelmed. As I sat there listening to the music with closed eyes, the Lord did not communicate with me verbally, but I had a profound sense that I was in His presence and before His throne. He didn't have to say anything—His presence was enough. I did not want this awesome experience to end. Peace came over me, and I went to sleep.

The next morning, June 5, I got on my bike to ride out and have my devotions by Boulder Creek. As I was riding down the road, I noticed a pornographic magazine, discarded in plain view on the shoulder of the road. The sight of that magazine scared me, because I didn't want anything like that near me. I stopped, grabbed the magazine, rolled it up, and stuck it in the pack on the back of my bike. I rode as fast as I could to Boulder Creek, and once there, hurled it as far out into the water as I could.

I am so thankful to God that He helped me to do that that day. It was the day God had chosen for Jason to die.

I rode up into a landing in the clear-cut and opened my Bible. For decades, I have followed a read-through-the-Bible-in-a-year plan. I opened the guide up to June 5 and there was directed to read the fifteenth chapter of John. I read verse 7: "If you remain in me and my words remain in you, ask whatever you wish, and it will be done for you".

Wow. This is what I read five years ago, when this started. And here I am again. I finished my quiet time and rode back home, not telling anyone what had happened nor what Scripture I had read.

That day was sports day at school, and Sherrie and I had planned to go watch Matthew because Jason's much-loved and dedicated teacher had volunteered to drive to our house to sit with him. She was out in the trailer with him, and we were in the house getting ready to go, when we heard her call on the intercom. "Could you guys come out here? Jason wants to talk to you right away."

We ran outside and asked, "What is it, Jason?"

He stared at us with wide eyes and said, "Somebody tapped me on my shoulder."

"Who was it?" I asked.

"I don't know." He fell asleep and became unresponsive. Suddenly, he raised his head again, eyes huge. "He tapped me again. Somebody tapped me again, on my shoulder."

I said, "Who?"

"I don't know. I don't want both of you to go to town. Mom, would you stay with me?" Then he fell asleep again. The third time this happened, he became excited. "Dad, somebody tapped me on my shoulder."

I was perplexed. "Is it scaring you?"

Jason instantly reassured me. "Oh, no. No, it's good!" Then he went to sleep again.

That was the last thing Jason ever said to me. I went to town to watch Matthew; Sherrie stayed with Jason. I am so grateful that Sherrie stayed behind.

Early June 1996.

God, Heal Jason Right Now!

I WATCHED MATTHEW at his sports day and afterward took him out for a snack. As we were sitting at a table in a restaurant, I asked, "Are you worried about your brother?"

"Yeah." Matthew had just turned twelve.

"You know, he's all right."

"I know he's OK. I know that if he died, he would just go to heaven. But Dad, can't we just ask God to heal him right now?"

"We have been asking God to heal him, Matthew."

"Yeah, but can't we ask Him today, to do it right now?"

"Yes, we'll stop and do that on our way home." I did a few errands around town, and we headed for home.

Partway out on the drive to Moricetown, we came to a scenic pull-out that gave a spectacular view of Hudson's Bay Mountain. I exited the highway, pointed our car toward the mountain and parked. "Do you want to pray that, Matthew?"

Matthew prayed very specifically. He prayed that God would heal Jason right at that very moment. He prayed that the cancer would never come back and that Jason would be happy and able to run around and eat, and that God would heal Jason right now.

Matthew expressed great faith by his words, and when he finished, I added, "Lord, I agree with Matthew. I leave that with You. I pray this in Jesus' name."

As we left, I glanced at my watch and noted the time: 3:43 p.m. We finished the drive home, and as we turned down our road, I could see my dad and Sherrie out ahead, standing out in the driveway. As soon as

I saw them both out there, I got a sinking feeling. I drove in, and Sherrie went right to Matthew's side of the car. She opened the door and said, "Matthew, Jason went to be with the Lord. He's in heaven."

"No, it can't be," Matthew said. "We just asked God to heal him. It can't be." He began crying and defiantly repeated that it couldn't be. I sat motionless in my seat, still holding on to the steering wheel, and cried. Sherrie came around to my door, and I got out and hugged her.

"When did Jason die?" I asked.

She said, "I don't know the exact minute, but it was between 3:40 and 3:45."

As we stood holding each other, crying, I was torn in two directions. While I felt tremendous grief, I also was relieved that Jason's suffering was over.

You Finished Well

I WALKED OVER TO the fifth-wheel to see Jason. My mom was already with him. When I saw Jason lying on the bed, I could tell right away he wasn't there. I went on my knees at the foot of the bed and cried. Mom told me that I should hold him, so I climbed up on the bed with him and held him in my arms.

I spoke aloud to him. "Jason, Jason, you finished well. You finished well." That was all I could think of to say. I was so sad, and yet I was so very proud of him. *Now your time of suffering is done. That is what I was concerned about. Now we can suffer missing you. But that's OK. I want to miss you—I want to have that pain, because you are special to me.*

As we sat beside Jason, our conversation turned to the fact that God could raise Jason from the dead if He chose to. We actually acknowledged this to God in prayer. "Lord, if it would honor You, if that is what You have for us to ask here, and it would honor You, we pray that You would raise him up. Otherwise, we accept what You are doing. We leave that in Your hands." Afterward, I remarked that I didn't think that Jason would want to come back to this body that he had been in. Turning to Matthew, I explained that God did do exactly what he asked in his prayer, exactly when he asked. Obviously, God's answer was not what we had expected. I affirmed that God did answer his prayer—in an even greater way than we imagined.

After a while, I tried to think what the next steps should be. Scott was at work in a local sawmill and needed to be picked up. We needed to call the hospital and tell them what happened. They would send out the coroner. We began by driving to the mill to pick up Scott and brought him home. The coroner was notified, and word quickly spread around Moricetown that Jason had died. Vanya and his mother came over, and both wailed in grief.

A short time later, the coroner and an assistant arrived with a body bag. We were told that we could go outside the trailer, and that they would take care of Jason's body. I knew what they were going to do and did not want them to bring him out to the coroner's vehicle in a bag. I told them that I wanted to carry him out myself. The coroner assured me I didn't need to do that. I affirmed that I knew that didn't need to do it, but that I wanted to. I was so proud of Jason. I picked Jason up and carried him outside to the waiting vehicle and laid him on top of the body bag. I felt like I was carrying a valiant soldier home from the battlefield. Moments later, the coroner took him away.

We stood in the driveway feeling like a huge piece of our life was suddenly missing. Jason was not there. So much of our life the past five years had been consumed by caring for him. All that had changed in an instant, leaving a huge void. We were thankful that Jason's suffering was over, and because God had taken him at the same moment that Matthew had prayed, we knew God's hand was in all of this. This knowledge was a profound comfort.

Even before the coroner left our driveway, people from Moricetown began to gather in our yard. People stepped forward, wrapped their arms around us, and began to plan the next steps. We felt enveloped by the community in a deeper way than we had experienced before.

A week before this, I had been visited by Victor Jim, Jason's former principal and one of the Moricetown elders. He had said, "Doug, I've been talking to some of the elders. Our desire is that you never need to hear this, and nothing is ever going to happen, but if Jason were ever to die, we want you to feel free to come to us to bury Jason in the traditional way if you would like to do that." Shortly after Jason died, I called Victor and told him that we would be honored to have Jason buried in the traditional way. Victor replied, "OK. I'll take care of it from here."

In the traditional Wet'suwet'en way, Victor stepped in and took over making the arrangements from there. From that point, the only decision Sherrie and I had to make was the selection of the casket. We chose a simple, unfinished casket, designed to provide a good surface for people to write tribute messages on.

In keeping with the cultural patterns in Moricetown, we had a memorial service at our house. Many kids who knew Jason attended and wrote personal memorials to him on the outside of the casket. The following day, the funeral service was held at the largest church in Smithers. The seating capacity of six hundred was grossly exceeded, with people standing in the halls and out the doors. Included in those attending were the manager and several others from Ronald McDonald House who had made a great personal effort to come up from Vancouver.

At Scott's insistence, we began the funeral by playing a CD of the song *If You Could See Me Now*. Because of the overcrowding, a large number of people had gathered outside the church and were singing songs while they waited to make their way inside. There was an atmosphere of joy, unlike that of any funeral I had ever attended. One of our mission board members presided over the funeral proceedings, which included numerous speakers and testimonials. A book of tributes collected before the funeral was printed and circulated. One of the testimonials that stood out for me was from Jason's friend Vanya. Vanya wrote, "To my best friend. One thing I remember about Jason is all the times we were going to do something not very good. He would try to stop us, or just walk away. He was one of the best friends I ever had, and I am going to miss him very much.

Following the funeral, we drove in procession for the interment at the Moricetown Cemetery. We traveled over a stretch of highway where you can see probably two or three miles. We were in the lead car, following the hearse, and as I looked back over my shoulder, I saw the funeral procession reaching back as far as I could see. It is impossible to describe how much it meant to me for so many people to just be there. At the interment, a simple wooden marker that I had made was erected, intended to serve until the gravestone would be set a year later, as is the cultural tradition in Moricetown. Jason's death feast was held the following day, with most of Moricetown in attendance.

The Beginning of the Real Story

A YEAR LATER, we began to prepare for the headstone feast, the occasion that traditionally marks the end of the year of mourning. We had one last decision to make—the script on the gravestone. Matthew knew what he wanted written. As a family, we had read C. S. Lewis's Chronicles of Narnia. In the last volume, *The Last Battle*, Aslan is seen talking to the kids, who do know that they died in a railway accident and are now in the heavenly, real Narnia. Colors are more vibrant and everything is more real than they have ever experienced. Aslan explains to the children that there really has been a railway accident, and things have fundamentally changed. "The term is over: the holidays have begun. The dream is ended: this is the beginning."[1] Lewis concludes the book with these words:

"For us this is the end of all the stories, and we can most truly say that they all lived happily ever after. But for them it was only the beginning of the real story. All their life in this world and all their adventures in Narnia had only been the cover and the title page: now at last they were beginning Chapter One of the Great Story which no one on earth has read: which goes on forever: in which every chapter is better than the one before."[2]

Inspired by this passage, and at Matthew's insistence, Jason's headstone is inscribed with these words: "This is just the beginning of the real story."

I believe this truly is just the beginning of the real story. It is so

---

1   Lewis, C. S. (1976). *The Last Battle*. New York: Puffin Books, page 165.
2   Lewis, C. S. (1976). *The Last Battle*. New York: Puffin Books, page 165.

apparent to me now that Jason's life was not cut short in any way. On the basis of Psalm 139:16, I believe that before Jason was born, his thirteen and a half years of life on earth were recorded in God's Book of Life. In reality, his life, the life that God has given him, is no shorter than anyone else's. Jason continues to live with the Lord—and will continue to live forever. That knowledge is a great help and comfort to us.

Two Vacations

THE SUMMER AFTER JASON DIED, we went on a vacation to Lac La Biche, Alberta. A local fisherman I knew gave us tips as to where the fish congregated at that time of year, and by following his instructions carefully, we located a weed bed where, over several days, we caught hundreds of northern pike. Although we missed Jason, it was a special, fun time with our family.

We especially looked forward to sunset. Each night, we went out on the beach, and the northern lights were unlike anything I have ever seen. God had given us this great time together. I was reminded of Psalm 90:15, in which the psalmist implores God, "Make us glad for as many days as you have afflicted us, and for as many years as we have seen trouble". I believe that God did that at that particular time and has continued to a number of times since.

I am so thankful that even at the some of the lowest points in Jason's journey, when I started to think about what it would be like to trade places with someone else, I could always say, "No. This is where God wants me to be. He doesn't make mistakes. This is the best—for all of our family." I continue to believe that.

The second summer after Jason died, Sherrie, Matthew, and I joined Mom and Dad in camping at Agate Beach on Francois Lake. While there, we met a couple in their seventies. As we got to know them, we learned that many years before, their son died at age thirteen from Ewing's sarcoma, just like Jason. This couple was still so bitter; all they could think about was their son's death. They told us it would never get better, it would only get worse. We tried to share with them about our faith and about Jason's faith and the hope we had. They just said, "No, no, it will only get worse."

We were not better people than they in any way. Being better or stronger had nothing to do with it. We had a hope that they didn't have, and that hope is what made the difference. Without that hope, we would be where they were, or even worse. I realized then the difference that knowing the Lord makes.

Grieving

IT WAS HARD AFTER JASON DIED. We missed him so. While I didn't feel angry with God, emotionally my cup was full. My temper was frayed, and minor annoyances would trigger uncharacteristic rage.

One night, I went out to the car after dark to find something. I could not find what I was looking for, and this insignificant frustration sent me into a rage. I hurled my still-lit flashlight across the road into the hay field. I just stood there in the dark, looking at the glow of the flashlight out in the hay field. *That was really smart. Now you've got to go out there and get the flashlight.* As I climbed over the fence and walked out to where the flashlight lay, I was thankful that no one had witnessed this display.

On another occasion, while in my woodworking shop, I hit my thumb with a hammer. I responded by hurling the hammer with all my strength into the floor. When this sort of thing happened, I realized that my grief was affecting me more than I thought. Even though I felt like I had accepted what God had done, these emotions would come over me—sometimes in waves. There would be days when I was doing fine, and then suddenly I would break down and cry.

In the years following, there were times when I thought I was pretty well finished with grieving, only to discover I was not. On one occasion, I was at Peace River Bible Institute, talking with someone about one part of the story. Totally unexpectedly, I became overwhelmed. A flood of tears came, and I could not speak. Several years after Jason died, I went back to Ronald McDonald house for a visit, confident that my grief was behind me. As I walked through the front door, a momentary but powerful flood came over me. I had planned to visit people that I knew were there, but I could not. I just could not enter the building. I hurried back to my car and sat and cried.

One of the seedlings we planted that first day that we learned of Jason's illness is thriving in our backyard. It has grown into a beautiful specimen of a lodgepole pine, nearly twenty feet tall. The other seedling died. I don't know if there is any great significance to that, but the tree that remains is a constant reminder of Jason, while the seedling that died reminds me of Jason's twin, Michael. When we planted those seedlings, I prayed that the trees would grow to be tall and strong, and that Jason would too. Although Jason's life was short, his life has made a profound impact on our family and community. The legacy of his life is tall and strong.

Epilogue

SHERRIE, SCOTT, MATTHEW, AND I have shared this story of hope many times. I cannot count the number of people I have shared the Gospel with using Jason's story. As the years go by, opportunities continue to come up—often in surprising ways.

About a year ago, I picked up a young man who was hitch-hiking on the highway near Moricetown. Although I didn't recognize him when I first pulled over, I soon did.

As we drove along, my passenger mentioned his age. I told him I had a boy who would have been his age, but he had died. My passenger expressed his sorrow. He asked how old my son was when he died. I said he was thirteen when he died of cancer, but I added that he was ready to die because he knew the Lord. As I started to share Jason's story, my passenger stopped me. He said, "Wait a minute. Who are you? What is your son's name?"

I replied, "Doug Anderson. My son's name was Jason."

My passenger disclosed his name, which I immediately recognized. The last time I had seen my passenger, he was eight years old, had no hair, and was battling leukemia. He had been one of Jason's three room-mates when we first went to Children's Hospital in Vancouver. As we talked, I discovered that he had just been released from jail in Smithers and was heading home. While in jail, someone had given him a book containing testimonies of First Nations Christians, and now he found himself riding with Jason's dad, having this conversation. "This is freaking me out!" he exclaimed.

"It should freak you out," I said. "It's freaking me out too. God wants to speak to you—I believe He's talking to you now. You just read that book, and although I haven't seen you for fifteen years, I picked you up today. What are the odds of that?" As we continued to talk, I challenged him to follow Christ. The drive was an incredible experience for me, and I saw again that God is still working in and through those difficult experiences.

Years before I told God to do what He needed to do to bring people to Himself. When I sensed Him saying, "Doug, even if it means taking your son home? Even if it means that?" I left it with Him. Even though God chose to take Jason, I have no regrets.

Jason's legacy has profoundly impacted those closest to him. When Matthew was baptized, he read his testimony publicly. Neither Sherrie nor I had realized it before, but Matthew testified that the reason he is a Christian is because of Jason's life. In Jason, he saw the reality of Christian faith lived out. While it wasn't the only purpose, Sherrie and I are confident that Jason's illness was God's way to open Matthew's eyes to Himself. At least to some degree because of his experience of Jason's illness, Matthew is going to be in heaven.

This knowledge helps dispel some of the whys. That is not to say that Sherrie and I don't still have times of questioning. We do. That's one of the reasons we keep Jason's picture beside a plaque with Churchill's famous exhortation in clear view on the bookcase beside our telephone. We and everyone who walks into our living room are continually reminded of Jason's emphatic admonition to us: "Never give up!"

When we set Jason's permanent headstone, I carried the simple wooden cross I made as his first grave marker up to the summit of Mt. Seaton, the nearest peak in the beautiful mountain range we look at from our yard. I set the cross up in a rock cairn, and from time to time I return there for prolonged quiet times with the Lord. From this vantage point, the magnificent Bulkley Valley spreads out between the perpetual snowcaps of the surrounding mountain ranges. I love to go back to this place and a number of times have met the Lord there in significant ways.

Sherrie and I miss Jason, painfully. Scott and Matthew miss their brother deeply, as do many others. We all cling to the hope we have in Christ. We are confident that a thousand years from now, we will look back at this and praise God for His wisdom, goodness, and providence, and yes, even to thank Him for allowing Jason to contract Ewing's sarcoma. In the meanwhile, we consciously work at being thankful. We continue to learn to trust God—not because we are strong, but because He is.

"Soli Deo Gloria!"